RE

Charlotte M. Goodman
2600 SE Ocean Blvd., Apt. E-14
Stuart, FLORIDA 34996-3416

Don'T Put me In
a Nursing Home!

RE

Revised Edition
- 4th PRINTING -

Dr. Amarnick responds to every elder's silent plea:

"DON'T PUT ME IN A NURSING HOME!"

Claude Amarnick, D.O.

Updated by Arnold S. Goldstein, J.D., LL.M., Ph.D.

Published by Garrett Publishing, Inc.
384 S. Military Trail
Deerfield Beach, Florida 33442
All rights reserved

©1996 Claude Amarnick — *first printing 06/96*
©1997 Claude Amarnick — *second printing 03/97*
©1999 Claude Amarnick — *third printing 06/99*
©2001 Claude Amarnick — *fourth printing 01/01*

"Don't Put Me in a Nursing Home!"
Library of Congress Catalog Number 96-077342
Claude Amarnick, D.O.
Deerfield Beach, Florida
188 pages
ISBN 1-880539-38-1: $13.95

Cover design by Lloyd MacDonald

Praise for
"Don't Put Me in a Nursing Home!"
by Dr. Claude Amarnick

his excellent book addresses issues which are becoming more and more important as our population advances into old age and family support structures fragment. Nursing homes and institutions for the elderly are one option, but a civilized society can be judged by (among other things) the way it cares for its elders. Dr. Amarnick makes a strong and compelling case for saner, more compassionate ways of dealing with the issues which aging can bring. Highly recommended.

Leon Chaitow, N.D., D.O.
SENIOR LECTURER, UNIVERSITY OF WESTMINSTER, LONDON, ENGLAND
EDITOR, JOURNAL OF BODYWORK AND MOVEMENT THERAPIES,
CENTER FOR COMMUNITY CARE AND PRIMARY HEALTH,
UNIVERSITY OF WESTMINSTER

ssential road map with clear, lucid choices for all those interested in providing a quality of life for our vulnerable, older family members.

Unfortunately, there will always be a need for nursing homes for some. But for many of us, this book can provide happier alternatives for our elders.

Ernest M. Weiner, D.P.M.
DIRECTOR, BOARD OF DIRECTORS
THE JOSEPH L. MORSE GERIATRIC CENTER,
WEST PALM BEACH, FLORIDA

*D*r. Amarnick's skills will pick up the cudgel and carry on. Dr. Amarnick's book is a wonderful kick in the pants to give Americans back their independence and sense of responsibility for themselves and their families. God bless your endeavors.

George Page
SENIOR VICE PRESIDENT, PAINE WEBBER

I strongly believe that this is an idea whose time has come. We have an opportunity to make a significant impact on our health care system by getting this information to millions of people who sorely need it.

Frank G. Antonino, D.C., DAAPM, ABFE
BOARD CERTIFIED PAIN MANAGEMENT SPECIALIST
AMERICAN ACADEMY OF PAIN MANAGEMENT
BOARD QUALIFIED CHIROPRACTIC NEUROLOGIST
AMERICAN BOARD OF FORENSIC EXAMINERS

I've had a look through Claude's book and it certainly appears to be a winner. I wish you every success in this new venture.

Betty Schwartz,
HOODER & STOUGHTON PUBLISHERS, LONDON, ENGLAND

A perfect prescription for caring for today's elderly. Packed with practical tips for dealing in the real world problems of caring for the elderly.

Arnold S. Goldstein, J.D., LL.M., Ph.D.

A strong and compelling case of dealing with our aging population. MUST READING!

Mario D. German, Esq.

D r. Amarnick is a truly remarkable man to have written such a book. Nobody could have written this book without dealing with chronically sick people. That takes a lot of understanding, warmth and love. Besides being a great physician, Dr. Amarnick was obviously able to look into their hearts and feel their anguish.

Sylvia Karpo
PHILADELPHIA, PENNSYLVANIA

D r. Amarnick has written a very supportive and helpful book for the elderly and their carers, confronting a major and increasingly important problem in our society and providing alternatives for serious consideration.

Martin Collins, Ph.D., C Biol, D.O., MRO
THE BRITISH SCHOOL OF OSTEOPATHY, LONDON, ENGLAND

Acknowledgements

This book was made possible through the generosity of neighbors, friends, patients, elders, caregivers, professionals, family members, confidantes, and role models who opened their lives and their hearts in order to spread the message: Growing old at home should be an option for every elder.

To Dr. Arnold S. Goldstein, who never hesitated to offer his expertise and professional know-how. This book, which we hope will help everyone, would not have happened without the professional guidance and hard work of Dr. Goldstein. Thanks will never be adequate for the services rendered from start to finish.

To editor Candice Richard, who labored many hours on this manuscript and came to know the author's thoughts and words as though they were her own. She cradled the manuscript from beginning to completion to hone the words.

To Lloyd MacDonald and Ginny Holm, for turning pages of manuscript into the book you are holding.

To Beverly Sanders, Hilary Lloyd, Susan Denoto, and all the professionals at Garrett Publishing for their professional efforts.

To the Broward County (Florida) Area Agency on Aging and the thousands of similar organizations that add so much to the lives of elders across the nation.

Thanks to you all!

This book is written for old people and people planning to be old, for caregivers and people planning to be caregivers. For simplicity I refer to the old person, whether spouse or parent, friend or lover, self or other, as the "elder," and, in the third person, as "he." I refer to the "family caregiver," whether daughter, grandson, friend, or husband, as "she." This is a writer's crutch and does not imply that the reader may not be the elder; that the elder may not be a parent, sibling, dear friend, spouse or lover; that only men grow old or that only women give care.

"Don't Put Me in a Nursing Home!" A book written by a Dr. of Psychiatry, Physiatry —physical medicine & rehabilitation—and Gerontology.

"Don't Put Me in a Nursing Home!" is NOT an advertorial for long term care insurance! When the book is perused or read, the need for long term care insurance for themselves or their ageing parents, relatives or friends, becomes a must issue in their minds and planning.

Though the title and much of the book deals with home care, the author states "This is not the continuum of care for a small subset of the very frail and sick-elderly individual."

"Don't Put Me in a Nursing Home!" clearly states you MUST prepare for the long term care.

By having long term care insurance, your probability of staying OUT of a nursing home is greatly enhanced.

The book's basic philosophy is growing old at home should be an option for every elder. Long term care planning may be the most important benefit of all pre-retirement plans.

The author takes on this frightening yet timely topic. Challenging elders and their families to begin realistically assessing every option that can keep a loved one out of a nursing home when they are able to utilize home care...however, again, this is not to deny the role of the nursing home—there is a need for this type of care!

"Don't Put Me in a Nursing Home!" Educates the elder, the care giver and society as a whole!

Education is the motivation—unless you know why something is likely to happen, you won't take measures to protect yourself.

Table of Contents

WHAT IF IT WERE YOU? 1

More likely than not, you will one day land in a nursing home.

Is the above statement just one more statistic or a horrific prediction that fills you with cold dread?

The prospect of aging terrifies most Americans. And our #1 worst fear? Not the prospect of a stroke or Alzheimer's disease, as you might suppose. Not a bleak future as a loved one's financial burden. A 1991 survey conducted by the Alliance for Aging Research says our greatest fear is spending the end of our life in a nursing home. And the closer we get to "old age," the more fearful we become. As one elder aptly remarked, "Aging hasn't bothered me a whit; what I worry about is a nursing home."

A nursing home strikes many of us as a sterile halfway house to the mortuary. We fear abuse, bad food, poor care. We worry about lost savings, lost independence, our very lives lost to second-rate nursing home care.

To America's elders, the nursing home is a life sentence to mental and physical imprisonment. Once inside, we are convinced, we will have little or no control over such basic daily decisions as when to get up in the morning, what to eat for breakfast, and how to spend the afternoon.

Our perceptions are so horrendous that some people become hysterical even when temporarily confined to a nursing home. Elders rightfully believe that institutionalization is the prelude to death. Those with children also perceive it as rejection by those who should most love and want to care for them.

The fear is understandable. Today's generation of grandparents and great-grandparents was the first to see their own elders typically survive into their 70s. They anguished over sending their parents to nursing homes 20 or 30 years ago. Now that they face a similar fate, they are determined not to go.

Anything but that!

So the elderly are opting for alternatives—although not necessarily better alternatives. Along with some excellent residential plans for those who can afford them, our elders are choosing hovels, abuse, the street, bus stations, and isolation in their own homes. Today's elders will do almost anything to avoid a nursing home.

Studies prove that fear of a nursing home is a major cause of suicide among the elderly. The University of Washington in Seattle reviewed suicides taking place over a 12-month period in one county. Fear of ending up in a nursing home overshadowed depression, chronic illness, and pain as reasons for taking your own life.

Almost as drastic are elders who become hermits in an effort to stay out of institutions. Long beyond the point where they can maintain the house or care for themselves, they remain closed in at home, frequently in deplorable conditions, willfully isolated from friends or a helping hand. Officially termed "self-neglect," this is the most prevalent form of elder abuse reported today.

"Often they don't want to give up the one thing in life they can control—where they live," says Linda Vinton, assistant professor at Florida State University's School of Social Work.

Imagine yourself in their place. Imagine abandoning your independence and entering a world of very old people, all of them frail and needing protective care. There is no escaping this world. All hope of an extended, gratifying, and self-controlled future is lost. Reminders of your physical deterioration are everywhere: your roommates, those you pass in the halls, those who gather for meals or other activities. The staff is so preoccupied with nursing and medical care, they no longer see you as an individual. It is inevitable that you come to think of yourself as ill, aged, and unable to care for yourself

There is always damage when an older person enters an institution, no matter how clear the need or positive the conditions. Removing someone from familiar surroundings—even when those surrounding are crowded, dirty, or in some other way unacceptable—can create depression, confusion, and loss of contact with reality. The consequences include feelings of helplessness, separation from society, loss of human contact, and an increased likelihood of death.

Nursing homes have been defined as depressing environments that impose the worst features of institutional care upon those least able to resist. The possible effects on nursing home residents include:

1. Dependency

2. Depersonalization

3. Low self-esteem

4. Lack of occupation or productive use of time

5. Geographic and social distance from familiar people and ways of doing things

6. Inflexibility of routine

7. Loneliness

8. Loss of privacy

9. Lack of freedom

10. Infantilism

11. Desexualization

Studies show that each year between 250,000 and 500,000 Americans are assigned to long-term care institutions for reasons other than medical need. Between 48 percent and 62 percent of patients in skilled nursing homes could receive comparable care at home. In sum, they do not require the level of care received and/or could otherwise become ambulatory.

Misplacement becomes even more important when we add another fact: Those placed in a nursing home, even for the most minor reason, rarely move out of the institution and return to an independent life in the community.

Nor is it easier on the families of these elders. Given an elderly spouse who has been hospitalized and needs extensive nursing care, or a parent who seems less and less capable of caring for himself, a loving family faces an unenviable decision. The reluctance and guilt they feel partly reflects the very stereotype I have just described: the belief that nursing homes are warehouses for the sick and old.

Families must somehow justify that a parent or spouse who for years may have been a selfless caregiver is now to be abandoned to the care of strangers (albeit trained and competent), and often in the elder's time of greatest need.

"Don't Put Me in a Nursing Home!" is thus written for our elders and for all of us: their children, relatives, family caretakers, health care providers, friends, and anyone else interested in geriatrics.

Structuring a community

I set several goals for this book:

1. **To open** people's eyes to the possibilities and potential for approaching our elders' aging—and, one day, our own—in new ways.

2. **To enable** elders to stay healthy and functionally independent for as long as possible.

3. **To acknowledge** and offer support to families who want to care for their elders but find the responsibility overwhelming.

4. **To make accessible** whatever short-term, long-term, and terminal care is required as our elders live longer and increase in number.

5. **To provide** that care in the least restrictive, most cost-effective and appropriate environment possible with as much patient responsibility as our American social service system can muster.

In practical terms, this book shows you how to structure a "community" and home environment to maintain the health and independence of the elder you love.

Nearly 35 million Americans are over age 65. They will more than double to 70 million people over the next 40 years, according to the U.S. Census Bureau. By then, the population of people

85 and over—the fastest-growing demographic group in America—will have almost tripled to nearly 9 million. These elders represent a significant slice of our population that deserves and demands a higher quality of life.

But while our senior citizens now constitute about 13 percent of the population, studies show they use 30 percent of the nation's health care resources and are responsible for 40 percent of all visits to internists. They account for 44 percent of all hospitalization days. Although 86 percent experience some form of chronic (long-term or recurring) condition, the good news is that 95 percent of our elderly continue to live in the community; approximately 80 percent without extensive assistance!

Some 6.5 million elders live alone, many with supportive loved ones nearby. Those with a family and access to assistance are more likely to be cared for at home, even when they have the same disabilities as most nursing home residents. In fact, a specific "social support" system—a spouse, child, and/or community services—substantially reduces an elder's chances of a nursing home stay.

Clearly, the reason so many elders end their days in nursing homes is the lack of supportive services. I believe that only those who need 24-hour care would be in nursing homes if occasional and temporary self-care needs could be provided in the community.

Many elders can maintain independence with only select services. Access to transportation may be enough to ensure independence, or regularly scheduled visits from someone outside the home. An occasional house call from the family physician might be necessary for an elder who needs periodic reassurance of medical care and surveillance. Day hospital care may be required for those with greater daily medical and social needs.

In a perfect world

In a perfect world, elders could elect services and still maintain their homes and their autonomy. But such arrangements are not readily available in most regions of the country, so many elders cling to independent living—the only alternative, as they see it, to institutional care. Ironically, the results are usually the opposite of what they hoped for. These seniors, confined to home and avoiding any community services for fear of being "found out" or "sent away," deteriorate faster. They are faced with the nursing home question the very first time their independence is threatened by accident, illness, or change in their support system.

Not surprisingly, the elders most in jeopardy are the "old old"— 75 or older—who have minimum support. They tend to be widows, at that stage of life when there are almost three women for every man. Statistics reveal that this 75-plus widow has children whom she interacts with frequently, but they are themselves too old to meet the many needs of their dependent mother.

Even when blessed with dedicated and responsible children, this woman typically fears that her own deterioration or changes in her fragile social support system will mean institutionalization. The triple threat of separation, rejection, and the dreaded institutionalization are often perceived as abandonment, as separation from someone who has chosen to leave her.

Finding alternatives

To live through eight or nine decades means inevitable physical deterioration and social loss. When efforts to adapt to problems fail, elders and their families are forced to find alternatives. And in the waning 20th century, one of the few alternatives to independent living is institutionalized care. With each advancing year, every elder in America becomes more aware that catastrophic illness or the loss of social support will necessitate nursing home care.

Although "eldercare" is a new word and a new concept, over 20 percent of today's work force, about 120 million strong, expects to assume eldercare responsibility for parents or other seniors over the next three or four years. By 2005, 37 percent of U.S. workers will be ages 40 to 54, the prime years for caring for elderly parents. Conservatively, one in three of us will care for an elder by the year 2020.

Society is unprepared for this demographic revolution. Those 85 or older who will rely on their children will nearly double by 2030, and triple by 2050, the Census Bureau forecasts. Again, families will provide 80 percent of the eldercare.

Nursing home phobia spreads as the odds increase that our elders will end up in one. In the past two decades, more women entered the work force, and fewer adult children of aging parents were willing or able to care for their elders at home. Often, adult children live too far away to be of help.

Their first crisis thrusts an elder's family into a bureaucratic maze. They try to make care arrangements in the badly fragmented long-term care system that exists in America today. When the working caregiver lives 100 miles or more from the elder (in about half the cases), efforts are more futile.

Increased life expectancy also plays a huge role. Men of 65 will live another 15 years; women at 65 can look forward to another 19. About 43 percent of those now 65 will eventually enter a nursing home, up from 37 percent only six years ago, according to U.S. government forecasts. The price tag? About $30,000 per year per patient, paid for by the patient, the family and, of course, more and more by the taxpayer.

This is our challenge in providing alternative care for our elders.

America has historically had a custodial attitude toward its elders, making institutional care the most readily accessible medical service available today. Nursing homes are seen as the solution. But today, amid rising concerns about the quality of life in our old age, warehousing our elders is no longer acceptable.

The right answer will be different for every individual and every family. Inevitably, it lies in a combination of home health care services, eldercare centers, and community-based outreach services, all professionally directed and all of the highest quality. Most important, it must be cost effective.

Why today? What makes home health care the most viable and inviting option for families in the new millennium who want to keep an elder at home? Six reasons:

1. New government policies

2. Medical technology

3. The growth of HMOs and PPOs

4. Increased awareness of how we "health ourselves"

5. The growing fear of nursing homes

6. The growing emphasis on tender loving care

Perhaps we must view our golden agers through the Golden Rule: Do unto your elders as you would have your children do unto you!

Ira

"I've already told my wife: When it's that time for our parents, we bring them into our home. Nursing homes are for when there is no family left."

Ira Goldsmith believes his patients do well because they are in their own environment. "They go into a nursing home and they go down hill; they die of a lack of will to live," he says.

Ira has been a visiting nurse for 10 years, but he's also worked in a hospital and in a nursing home. He says the future is home care. In fact, he and another nurse are banking on it: They hope to start a private home care management business, something that isn't available in the southeastern part of the country.

"Medicare doesn't cover it, and neither do HMOs. But here in Florida we have a lot of older patients whose children are out of state. They want someone to see that medications are being taken, that there is food in the refrigerator, that the various services they're paying for are taking place. That's case management.

"As a visiting nurse, I might go into the home of a confused patient on Monday and pre-pour all his medications for him. I go back on Thursday and not one has been taken. He's perfectly capable of getting to the grocery store, but he can't seem to manage his meds. The family asks a neighbor to oversee the medications, and it's a simple enough job, but how many neighbors want responsibility for a life-and-death matter like that?

"Or maybe I go into the home to teach an elderly diabetic to give himself insulin injections. And he flat out *refuses, says he's too old to learn to do that. And his elderly spouse can't do it, either.*

"Or say I notice in the normal course of a visit that one of my patients could enjoy a little more independence if she got physical therapy. So I ask the doctor for a PT evaluation, and bingo! A therapist is coming to her home.

"Those are small worries that are enormous if you're trying to care for your parent from another state. And sometimes it's the details that make the difference between staying at home or going into a nursing home.

"There's no telling how someone will age; they're all different. I have a woman patient who had a difficult family life and feels guilty about a lot of stuff. She just sits and waits for me to come three times a week to give her medications and listen to her. I think she feels worthless. I encourage her to find some mahjongg players in her condo, or take the bus to the mall and buy herself a dress, or spend a weekend with one of her kids. She's capable of doing all of that, but you'd never know it. Sometimes she'll proudly report that she did what I suggested, but it's like she did it for me, not for herself.

"Then I have an 88-year-old lawyer. He doesn't feel worthless. He's got a scrapbook full of memories, and was a daily bike rider and walker before he was hospitalized. He's always asking me when he'll be able to get back to exercise. It's almost like I have to hold him back until he's healed. But he'll be biking again, I can guarantee it.

"All they want is someone who is honest with them. Even when I have a dying patient, I ask him what he's thinking about. I talk about dying, bring it into my practice. They all tell me they love me, and it's because I'm real; I don't hide anything. I figure, that's the way I want to be treated when I'm old."

OUR ELDERS DESERVE BETTER

It is said that the quality of a civilization is judged by how it cares for its elders. In the Orient, the attitude toward aging is one of reverence. The elder's life experiences and wisdom are treasured. Although physical ability and beauty have faded, the elder nevertheless holds a distinguished place of importance within the family and in society.

America, on the other hand, is a youth-oriented society. "Old" is a negative, and the fear of becoming old, or appearing old, causes widespread anxiety. Elders, dismissed as poor, powerless, and valueless, are ignored, abandoned, or barely tolerated.

Americans do not easily accept life's natural events. We scramble desperately to avoid the appearance of advancing age and the inevitability of death. We think of our elders not as our mentors or superiors but as our inferiors. And once we internalize that idea, we can dehumanize them. Ignoring or incarcerating our elders in nursing homes, as though they were sheltered animals, becomes justifiable.

Why do we place people in institutions when they could be better cared for at home? We have noted the psychological and cultural forces in America that create the attitude: That the old are ugly and useless. That they are annoying and frightening because they remind us of our own mortality. That because they are old they are different, and therefore should be institutionalized. Hopefully you and tens of thousands of people like you will help change our national attitude toward aging.

Social support

What society labels "attitude toward aging" translates into social support in an elder's immediate community. As we age, social support becomes a valuable resource. Elders with strong social support cope better with stress—declining health, the loss of a spouse—than do those who lack such support.

When they do experience health problems, these elders frequently turn to those in their support networks for assistance with Activities of Daily Living, or ADLs. ADLs are all the things we learn to do as children to care for ourselves and that become habits as we grow up. We all spend time with ADLs:

- Moving about in bed

- Personal grooming

- Dressing and undressing

- Eating

- Using our hands

- Walking

- Using the toilet

An elder's disability is usually measured by the ADLs he can manage independently. Another common scale, for those less impaired, measures how many Instrumental Activities of Daily Living (i.e. shopping, managing finances) a person can perform alone.

Eighty percent of the elders who enter a nursing home require assistance with at least one ADL. Compared with people who are not ADL impaired, those with one or two ADL problems are twice as likely to be admitted to a nursing home. Multiple ADL impairments are an even stronger predictor of nursing home placement.

Along with ADL difficulties, the elders who enter nursing homes are more likely to be the "old-old," less likely to be currently married, and more likely to be living alone. Typically they have sensory deficits and nearly four chronic conditions.

Social support from family and friends moderates the effects of declining health and greatly reduces the risk of institutionalization. Social networks in the community promote less illness and longer life than does the isolation of institutional life.

In the community, family, neighbors, or friends can provide transportation, shopping trips, and meals. Formal community support can include Meals on Wheels, congregate dining sites, telephone reassurance, friendly visitors, and the popular senior centers. With the addition of skilled health care provided by home care organizations, there is no reason why most elders can't remain in the community to enjoy a healthy and happy old age.

Environment

Environment also impacts the health and wellness of our elders. Environment includes immediate living space, the community, and our larger social system.

For some elders, their home is the environment they have functioned in for decades, perhaps a lifetime. The only change is in their abilities, needs, and interests within that environment. Other elders' home environments have changed dramatically, to smaller apartments, the homes of adult children, or nursing homes. New environments require a whole new set of skills and a new frame of reference for living.

In either case, to ensure the highest possible quality of life, the elder's immediate and external environment must be regularly assessed. Similarly, the resources and services that are available to him must be identified and updated.

We now recognize that some of the effects thought to be a consequence of aging are actually the result of a forced change of environment. For example, feelings of lessened well being, depression and high anxiety—the emotions often felt by nursing home residents—are associated with increased susceptibility to and slow recovery from disease. The conclusion: Nursing homes may be harmful to our health.

Ability and activity

Physical ability is a third factor governing an elder's quality of life. With age, our bodies weaken; we become increasingly susceptible to disability and illness. Elders, constantly reminded of this physical deterioration, must come to terms with:

1. Diminished physical capability

2. A growing awareness of vulnerability and mortality

3. A sense of helplessness that cannot be overcome, however forceful or intelligent the action

4. A need to rely upon others

5. A loss of independence

Many elders find this reality intolerable and resist any adaptation to limitations. This book explores these difficulties and helps the elder and his family caregiver find answers.

Finally, activity tells us how well an elder is managing the aging process. As a specialist in physical medicine and rehabilitation, I emphasize exercise. I stress the benefits of a well-defined and comprehensive exercise program throughout this book.

Activity becomes more meaningful to elders when it relates to an accomplishment or goal. Activities that most satisfy elders include entertaining friends, exercising, going outdoors, talking to others, and continuing or establishing hobbies. More than self-sufficiency, elders need good friends and involvement in many activities if they are to be happy.

Whether we are the community at large or an elder's specific social support, we can more effectively deal with our elders by working within their abilities and achievements. We must encourage them to be active and to maintain good support systems.

Isolation

Aging is inevitable from the moment of conception. How we react to the cumulative events of a lifetime are highly individual. There is a wide range of possible responses to the difficulties associated with advanced age.

At one end of the spectrum is the elder who simply will not give in. This is the survivor. Vigor and perseverance are prominent characteristics. Other elders are more likely to disengage, or withdraw from society. It is a natural phasing out of feelings, activities, and social ties, and is as normal as winding down after a long day.

How elders feel about being alone varies from acceptance to fear and depression. For some, contact with others is a priority, outweighing all other considerations. Elders occasionally insist on solitude. In any group of isolated elders, many have always been loners, a consequence of individual personality traits and behavior patterns. Loners have an advantage when they face the social deprivation common to older people. Although they, too, face the increased isolation of old age, their lives have always been independent. They can better deal with solitude than elders recently deprived of a spouse or close friend.

It is dangerous when psychological distress and regression accompany an elder's isolation. It should be countered immediately; the longer psychological distress is allowed to exist, the more unlikely the possibility of reversal.

How do we relieve social isolation? The critical question becomes: Does the elder wish to withdraw from people and activities, or is he forced to withdraw by conditions beyond his control?

To provide social support for elders, many programs have been developed that increase elder mobility or bring visitors to the elders. Transportation systems, for example, are a significant part of most socialization programs. But any such program must meet the wishes of the elder. For most elders, programs that relieve loneliness are a blessing, but ultimately every elder must make the choice.

Isolation, whether natural or distressed, overt or unspoken, is an inevitable part of aging. Consider:

1. **High frequency of widowhood.** Because women live longer than men, of the 6.5 million people over age 65 living alone or with non-relatives, 5 million are women.

2. **Demographic patterns.** The fragmentation of the family and the frequency with which the young move away has led to widespread abandonment of our elders. They are left behind in decaying central cities and towns with few or no social services.

3. **The physical consequences** of aging make moving around difficult or hazardous.

4. **Attitudes** that make our elders feel foolish, unwanted, even guilty for being alive, and more comfortable hiding themselves away.

5. **Enforced retirement,** which results in fewer natural opportunities for human relationships, jobs, and acquiring money.

6. **The deaths of friends** and relatives and the consequent break-up of the elder's most immediate social support system.

Growing old is OK

Aging is not bad. Normal aging need not involve dizziness, confusion, forgetfulness, or incontinence. Cataracts, skin diseases, chronic ailments, and depression are not necessarily part of aging. Many people grow into old age naturally, comfortably, and disease-free.

Nor is declining mental ability inevitable. In fact, cognitive tests administered to a range of ages showed that 20 to 30 percent of the people in their 80s scored as well as those in their 30s and 40s—presumably the mental prime of life.

Generally, we can determine who in a group of working, middle-aged adults will have good mental functioning in old age. Indicators include:

1. A flexible attitude

2. High reading comprehension or verbal fluency

3. A successful career or other active involvement in life

4. Keen mental interests that continue after retirement

Although American society tends to lump all elders together, the opposite is true: The older the group, the more dissimilar they become. There are huge variations among our elders.

However, there are some commonalities. Among the chief concerns all elders share are quality health care, social and financial independence, family or a substitute support system, affordable and comfortable housing, and a society that welcomes healthy, productive elders. Every elder wants to be treated with dignity. Every elder wants to be recognized not for the burden he places on others but for his past contributions and untapped potential.

Old age brings changes, just as the toddler, teen, and midlife years do. There is a slowing down of the body's systems that varies from elder to elder. Aging has no precise timetable, so chronological age can be a very poor indicator of physical age.

On the bright side, there are now solutions to most of the health problems elders face. The first line of defense is preventing disease or injury and encouraging the best attitudes in elders.

Growing old gracefully requires accepting—accepting limitations we cannot change, accepting help when independence is no longer possible, accepting new ways of thinking and living when the old ways no longer work. These challenges can be discouraging. The elder who receives regular and sincere encouragement most successfully meets the challenges of aging.

Achieving the optimum

Every elder has his own optimum level of wellness. This can be achieved independently or with the assistance of caregivers, whether family, volunteers, or professionals. But you cannot achieve the optimum in fragments. A holistic approach—looking at the person as a whole entity—is mandatory for an elder to achieve his optimum.

A holistic approach to aging considers the elder's past and current habits and lifestyle. The ups and downs of his life shape his perspective, which is irretrievably intertwined with his lifestyle and his personality. His ability to change as he ages involves self-concept, intellect, memory, and spirituality.

Spirituality, whether based on longstanding religious convictions or on an evolved sense of the meaning of one's life, often determines an elder's ability to hope, and hope is crucial to wellness. In fact, one of the emotional tasks of adjusting to old age and physical disability is to find the right balance between hope and realism.

I am convinced that there will come a day when the present nursing home concept can be all but dismissed. The goal must be for our elders to live independently, with greater autonomy and more opportunities for decision-making and activities. This self-care approach requires more flexible care and housing, but it can be and is being achieved.

Old-old is different

The outlook shifts slightly when you consider the old-old population Clearly, the 88-year-old elder is physiologically very different from the 66-year-old, but the ways in which they differ cause confusion. Are the two differentiated predominantly by chronological age, the way a 16-year-old and a 28-year-old differ? Or is the difference a function of infirmity? Are those with chronic illness and poorer health considered at risk? Does increased age alone define a high-risk group in need of enhanced screening? Comprehensive geriatric assessments are based on the assumption that function, health, and demographics identify high-risk elders better than does the age factor.

More than half our elders over 85 need long-term care. Ninety percent require help for the basic Activities of Daily Living. Caregivers are often a member of the family or a friend, and most frequently they are the spouse. Medicare recipients over 85 consume four times the services as do those between 65 and 69.

The old-old are also the critical age group for our $70 billion nursing home industry. With the graying of America, both the numbers of the old-old and the extent of their impairments will increase. In order to have enough quality nursing homes to serve those too frail to be elsewhere, a huge population of elderly in varying stages of dependency will need, want, and deserve to be cared for in the community.

Can the community answer the call?

Deirdre

"It's easier if it's sudden," says an exhausted Deirdre Ruhland, "but there's a blessing in having the chance to make the most of our time together. We have had so many warm and tender moments."

Deirdre's mother, Betty, has ALS, better known as Lou Gehrig's disease. Bedridden, no longer able to speak or eat, Betty is fed 6 hours every night through a tube. She has an attendant at her side 24 hours a day, as well as a devoted husband of 56 years, a son, and a daughter. If the disease progresses as expected, her muscle control will dissipate until she can neither breathe nor swallow.

"If we get four or five months," says Deirdre, "we're lucky.

"We made a family decision not to put her in a nursing home, no matter what," she adds. "And we're doing incredibly well. Mom has the best, most caring help. I know my mother is getting better support at home than she ever would in a facility."

It began with four hours of nurse's aides. Eventually Medicare was providing an aide every morning, seven days a week, along with physical, occupational, and speech therapists. But when Betty's improvement slowed to a halt, so did therapy. Now, in addition to the private home care, a nurse comes to start Betty's feeding tube every evening.

"It was taking me an hour to feed her a half-cup of cottage cheese," Deirdre recalls. "It tired her out, and she wasn't getting anywhere near enough calories. So we had to go with the tube.

"I'm afraid my mother has very little dignity left. Just getting her on the commode exhausts her. She won't allow her friends to visit anymore. She sleeps, she watches television, my father brushes her hair. She's trapped in a broken body with a perfect mind.

*"But when I walk into the room, her face lights up. And she can laugh, even though she can't talk. Isn't that wonderful? The other night we were watching **Ellen** on TV, and both of us were laughing just like we used to. It was delightful."*

Deirdre says there is excellent help for elders available through community services, but it's not intended for people as sick as her mother. In fact, hospice would come to take care of Betty at this point, but only if hospice is the sole provider. Neither Betty nor her family is ready quite yet to give up the private nurses that have become so important to her.

"Those women love my mother, and she loves them," Deirdre says, trying to explain the impact these strangers have had during this difficult period.

"One of the nurses lost her babysitter, and she was going to have to stay home to take care of her toddler. So we brainstormed, and made some accommodations, and Celia brought her daughter with her every day. It turned out to be a great decision. Marcy was a handful, but she brought life to our house.

"And she was the most sensitive two-year-old I've ever met. Marcy would see my mother alone in the living room, and she'd hold a Magic Marker like a microphone and sing and dance and entertain her, just the two of them. There wasn't a dry eye in the house. And she loved the alphabet chart we made to help my mother communicate. I have this mental picture I'll carry with me forever of a two-year-old and a dying woman, both of them struggling to meet the challenge of the alphabet chart, both of them learning to communicate in brand new ways.

"When this is over, that memory alone could sustain me. It's a reminder of the time we've had as a family since the onset of my mother's disease. And I guess it's a kind of confirmation that our family has done everything we can for my mother. How many families can say that?"

A WIN–WIN PROPOSAL

Home health care, once a small part of the nation's health care delivery system, is now one of its fastest growing fields. The market is growing by 12 percent annually. The home care market grew from $6.1 billion in 1986 to $13 billion in 1992 and to $19.5 billion in 1996.

Several factors account for the increasing use of home care. Hospital stays have shortened. Many patients who not long ago would have remained hospitalized following surgery or critical illness are being discharged earlier. Also, outpatient surgery has become more common, and patients do not need to remain hospitalized to receive treatment. Techniques and equipment once restricted to hospitals are now available for home use.

More than 7.1 million people received home health care in 1994, up from 5.9 million in 1987. According to the U.S. Commerce Department, home care and home infusion therapy (the services of nurses and aides and the intravenous delivery of drugs in the home) grew 35 percent in 1994. That's triple the growth of the rest of the health care industry.

The boom is due to the fact that home care is less costly than more traditional avenues of health care. A 1991 study compared the average cost of treatment of hip fractures, a common ailment treated through home care as well as in hospitals. It found that by discharging a patient six days earlier, $2,300 was saved. That translates into an annual Medicare savings of $575 million. Such savings, coupled with pressure from insurers to cut costs, is compelling hospitals to release patients sooner. And technological advances have made it possible to provide such sophisticated care as chemotherapy and respiratory therapy as easily in living rooms as in hospital rooms.

Home care can substitute for daily, comprehensive, hospital-level care as effectively as for less intense care. Elders rehabilitated safely and effectively at home include those with amputations, arthritis, stroke, hip fractures, total joint replacement, head injury, spinal cord injury, cerebro-vascular accident, neuromuscular disease, multiple sclerosis, and even pulmonary and oncological diseases.

Home health care programs not only provide these services, but they keep people out of nursing homes. The cost of home health care is about half that of maintaining the same population in nursing homes. And this includes rent, food, clothing, telephone, medications, professional health services, and the help of community services.

Demographics is another reason for the growing demand for home health care. In 1970, only 3.7 percent of the U.S. population was 75 or older. The Census Bureau projects that by the year 2000, 6.2 percent of the population will be 75 or older. In 2021 the baby boomers will begin to reach 75. This aging America offers a growing market for home delivery of a wide range of health and social services.

Lack of coordination

In 1982 the Tax Equity and Fiscal Responsibility Act (TEFRA) was legislated to contain increasing hospital health care costs by mandating cost reimbursement and length-of-stay requirements.

As a result, home health care services boomed as they attempted to serve a fragile population discharged early from the hospital into the community.

Most current home care programs rely on a patchwork of external funding sources: public programs (often through waivers of existing programs), grants, fee-for-services, hospital support. This patchwork reflects society's ambivalence toward funding these programs, presumably for fear of the costs.

A few communities have exceptionally well-organized programs to help elders and their families cope without excessive stress and strain. They are staffed by polite people who are willing and able to tell elders and their relatives what they must know. Many are free or reasonably priced.

Unfortunately, in most communities this is not the case; the need goes unmet. Families are likely to call all over town to dig for answers from an unconnected array of personnel, agencies, and companies linked somehow to long-term care. What is sorely needed is an organized, community-based service program throughout the country.

The goals are simple

A successful home health care program achieves two major purposes: It helps elders remain in their own homes—where they often desperately wish to stay—and it meets society's needs financially and in terms of support.

Nursing home beds and hospital beds are expensive. Home health services often prevent or delay transfer from the home to either. Home health care is uniformly accepted by elders, family caregivers, health professionals, policy makers, and the public as a desirable way to provide for the disabled and the elderly.

But such home health care programs can succeed only if there is clarity of purpose. For the elder, the goal is to stay out of an institution and in his own home at maximum independence. People generally prefer to live in their own homes. Elders feel good about a familiar environment. They can eat, watch television, sleep, and awaken on their own schedule. They can keep the lights on late and find the bathroom in the dark. Their independence is limited only by their frailty.

Home care provides the company of one's family, a less restrictive, more familiar environment, greater personal choice and dignity, greater patient participation, and a retained sense of usefulness. It enables the elder to maintain his activities, pets, and religious and ethnic customs. Confused or mildly demented elders who have lost the ability to process new sensations and information may be far more functional in their own homes than in a new environment.

For the community, the goal is to help families stay together, decrease the patients in nursing homes, and save public money.

For the health care industry, government, and business, the containment of health care costs has been the overriding concern of the 1990s. Mushrooming alternative delivery systems all claim to be cost effective. Home health care has become particularly attractive to self-insured businesses and the major third-party payers as an alternative to hospitalization because it delivers real savings.

For the consumer, greater self-responsibility for health care and increased knowledge have shifted interest back to home care.

Perhaps most importantly, home care is overwhelmingly accepted by the nursing profession, the professional caretakers who will form the backbone of the home care movement.

A host of financial advantages flow to the elder cared for at home. Although full-time skilled nursing care at home is expensive, the ability to select only essential services and to coordinate them with free community or volunteer programs reduces the overall cost considerably. And home care can be combined with day care and respite care, both less expensive alternatives to full-time institutionalization.

The brewing crisis

Long-term care, both in-home and institutional, merits greater attention than it has received. A crisis is brewing between the high and rapidly increasing costs of long-term care and the increasing demand for that care in the coming decades. Several symptoms are already visible:

1. The shortage of nursing home beds, evidenced by a growing difficulty in placing hospital patients into nursing homes and by the dilemma of families unable to care for severely disabled elders at home.

2. Widespread dissatisfaction with the compassion of nursing home care.

Richard Suzman, director of demographic studies at the National Institute of Aging, reports that "the geriatric consensus" among gerontologists once held that increased life expectancy would mean each of us could expect that a greater number of the years after retirement would be spent dependent on someone else for such basic Activities of Daily Living as taking a bath, getting dressed, going to the toilet.

Yet studies have shown that disability rates among the elderly have actually decreased during the past decade. Some factors include now-commonplace surgical techniques like cataract removal and joint replacement that allow the disabled to resume normal activities. Also a factor is that those who have retired since 1980 know and practice better nutrition and health care than those who preceded them.

Gerontology magazine reports that the number of elderly people requiring personal assistance declined 10 percent from 1982 to 1989—even as the elderly population increased! At the same time, those using mechanical aids but living independently without personal assistance increased 5 percent. Lower disability among the elderly may slow the increase in demand for costly nursing home care.

The same study indicated a substantial possibility for increasing our elders' activity. "For a lot of people with problems primarily related to joints, vision, or sensory function," it noted, "you could have biomedical intervention or nutrition therapy and have a larger potential for improvement."

The most important part of the study, according to Dr. Suzman, was the suggestion that disability was not an inevitable part of aging, and that it might be possible to find a way to slow or prevent such loss of function.

Prioritizing home health care for elders will permit elders to remain independent, save money for the larger community, help family members sustain their elders safely at home, decrease the number of nursing home patients the public must support, benefit the taxpayer when public health costs fall, and save money in health budgets. With results like that, the political establishment can honestly claim that they are both compassionate and thrifty.

Now *there's* a win-win proposal.

Rosemary

Eighty-five years ago, when Rosemary Davis was born in a rural New England town, she was so ill the doctor didn't think she would live to see her fifth birthday. In fact, she has lived to see her great-granddaughter's fifth birthday.

Fifteen years ago she and her husband left their beloved home town to follow their daughter and son-in-law to Virginia, where the younger couple had been transferred. Two years later Rosemary's husband of 53 years died suddenly. She has lived alone ever since. Rosemary has been hospitalized several times in recent years, including a gall bladder operation and gangrene of the appendix. At her daughter's suggestion, she has given up driving.

In many ways Rosemary fits the profile of elders most likely to need nursing home care. But statistics are superficial, and our elders are many-dimensioned. Anyone who sees Rosemary walking briskly through her neighborhood on her way to church, a smile and a friendly word for everyone she passes, would never guess she falls into society's category of "old-old." Certainly Rosemary doesn't see herself that way.

"I get up at 7:30 or 8 a.m. and have breakfast," Rosemary begins, recounting a typical day, *"and the next thing you know—knock! knock!—it's my neighbor coming to see if the coffee's on. Then maybe I'll join a group of women in the community who do crafts—I still make almost all my own clothes, and I dearly love to make dresses for my two great-granddaughters. Or I have a friend who loves the mall, and my daughter might drop us off over there for a few hours. We just walk and have lunch and browse.*

"Or I read, although my eyes aren't as good as they used to be. But I'm trying to read the Bible all the way through. And I work around the shrubs in the yard, or someone calls and asks me to go out. I never feel house-bound, and I try awfully hard not to waste my time.

"I've never been grouchy," Rosemary maintains. "I find life very interesting. I was a country girl, born on a farm, and I just wish every young person could have a country background, at least until age 12. A farm gives you a sense of security. The whole life circle was very beautiful to watch. There was always lots to eat and plenty of love. My mother was a Christian woman and my grandfather was a pastor. Who is around these days to steer children in the right way?"

Rosemary was a young married woman during the depths of the Depression, but again her background saw her through. "We always had a garden, and we survived," she says. "Sometimes the going got hard, but when we didn't have money we had roots."

Today her faith stands her in good stead. "If I get way down, I pick up my Bible and ask Him to help me. People say to me, 'You talk like He's real.' And He is! He's working on our behalf all the time. Sometimes I say to myself, 'Oh, boy, I can't handle this.' And then I think, 'Well, you don't have to handle it alone. You've got the Lord.'

"And I've got lots of energy, and I'm so grateful for that. And my HMO takes awfully good care of me. All my tests come up negative. Oh, I take water pills because there's too much fluid in my legs, and I take vitamins. But that's it, really.

"And I'm not often lonely. Sometimes, in the evening, I think, 'Oh, gee....' But then I tell myself, 'No, you can't think that way.' And in the morning there's that familiar knock! knock! and the start of another day."

HOW DOES IT FEEL TO BE OLD? 4

The consequences of aging range from changes in social roles and decreased satisfaction with life to an elder's progressive inability to care for himself or seek medical attention.

Potential physical danger to the elder or others can become significant when impaired functioning affects routine activities, like driving a car or preparing meals. A fierce determination to live may consume all his energy. His sense of inadequacy may contribute to feeling unlovable—and then he needs love more than ever.

Adjustment is a continuous lifetime process, of course, but old age encompasses acute mental as well as physical change. Some elders undergo changes in behavior; others lose the ability to adjust to change.

Consider the issues we all face as we age:

1. Financial distress: diminished or fixed income, medical and prescription bills, expenses for special care

2. Forced retirement and lost sense of purpose

3. Housing changes necessitated by diminished capabilities

4. Need for assistance in personal care

5. Diminished mobility, limiting independence and social-ization and requiring transportation alternatives

6. Need for new social contacts

7. Family problems created by the stress of aging

8. Loss of status: diminished self-esteem and importance in the eyes of others

9. Loss of loved ones as a consequence of death or geo-graphic separation

10. Isolation

11. Embarrassment over intellectual or physical disabilities

12. Diminished sexuality

13. Acceptance of oneself as elderly

14. Fear of death

These feelings can be reinforced by a spouse or family who may feel equally overwhelmed. Or they can be modified by sup-porters who mobilize positive feelings in themselves and the elder.

Add to this list of potential problems what I refer to as life cycle issues. These are roller-coaster changes that occur at vari-ous stages in the aging process and can include increased sensi-tivity to medication, increased physical frailty, and impaired cog-nitive function. The elder must also learn to accept changes in health and physical appearance and limitations in daily activities.

Making it even more difficult for both the elder and his fam-ily, the disabilities seldom occur in any set pattern or time frame.

These roller coaster issues involve a series of conflicts and resolutions that accompany periods of change and loss. Even as the elder and his family try to remain optimistic about recovery, they may become frustrated with the course and speed of the rehabilitation process. The overriding reality is that quality of life, rather than quantity of life, becomes the elder's chief health concern.

Isolation

Long periods of unwanted isolation, with absence of stimuli from the outside world, can result in anxiety, depression, agitation, or apathy and, ultimately, severe physical illness.

Elders who live alone often become saddened and unable to find joy in life. Disability such as arthritis or heart disease makes mobility more difficult, resulting in further physical or mental isolation. These elders see a future of increasing disability. Believing that no one cares about them, they withdraw even further.

This understandable feeling of being unwanted may spur defensive reactions. An elder may repel all efforts by others to establish closeness while, paradoxically, desperately wishing to be close. This ambivalence is an effort to protect against further rejection while wanting to participate in life's pleasures.

The physical self

Elders are stiffer, slower, and prone to aching joints and weak muscles. Osteoarthritis is probably the elder's major discomfort. Weakened muscles cause the elder to walk with feet farther apart, body swaying side to side in a rolling gait. Knees buckle; muscle weakness causes a sense of insecurity; sitting or rising from a chair is a major hurdle.

Each of us identifies strongly with our physical self, or, more precisely, with our perception of that self. Body image develops from birth and is conditioned not only by how we feel and what we see in the mirror, but by what others value in us. The body is a vehicle for the mind, with its intricate and endless possibilities for receiving, reordering, and communicating experience. An elder's body image includes all the skills and resources for enjoyment and for relationships with others that the body makes possible.

Body image helps determine whether illness, handicap, or mutilation diminishes or damages the self. It all hinges on the elder's self-respect. The ability to adapt to a radical change in appearance or body function depends on the value of that part in the total image of the self, the physical attributes that are tied to self-esteem and sense of security, and awareness of other resources. Adjustment is never easy and takes time.

Recovery sometimes requires restoring a positive self image. Because the self depends on the body in which that self has evolved, an elder may have to revise his personal definition of body and self.

Sense of identity

A severe handicap or life-threatening illness challenges a person's sense of identity. He may no longer see himself as a contributing member of society with useful skills. Instead, he sees himself as a liability.

He may be overwhelmed by negative feelings: bewilderment, self-pity, embarrassment, anger, hopelessness, worthlessness, discouragement, pessimism, and despair. He may lose pride in his accomplishments and in his capacity to carry once-familiar responsibilities. His confidence in the future may be damaged, as may his ability to enjoy what used to give him pleasure.

When a person believes that his actions no longer make a difference, he stops attempting to make a difference. Depression and an inability to make choices often accompany this "learned helplessness." One of the most distressing and debilitating aspects of incapacitating illness is the elder's sense of uselessness, of being detached from the world, unable to contribute or continue life on his own terms.

Still, faced with incapacitating illness, many patients—for reasons we don't fully understand—literally fight for life. People faced with radical limitations of accident or illness often discover untapped strengths that increase recovery rate or prolong their survival. Even a helpless, bedridden patient can, given opportunities for independence and initiative, maintain both self-respect and morale.

Personality changes

Personality changes may be dramatic with the chronically ill. Some elders with arteriosclerosis, rheumatoid arthritis, and other degenerative afflictions suffer permanent personality changes that are as serious as the underlying disease.

How he reacts to illness and aging depends largely on the elder's personality, inner resources, sensitivities, age, and illness. He may be stoic, or anxious that everything possible is being done, or afraid of "being a baby" while desperately needing basic care. He may be afraid to burden or frighten others. He may feel guilt, or fear rejection, for causing others distress.

By understanding the personality changes that illnesses produce, the caregiver and other family members can help the elder lead a productive and satisfying life—one that focuses on autonomy and personal initiative.

Range of feelings

Anyone, but especially an elder, may be resigned or challenged by the devastating effects of illness or incapacity. Illness may trigger old anxieties and unresolved conflicts. Or it may trigger previous successes in conquering difficulties.

Frustrated, hurting, unhappy elders can be irritable, demanding, or withdrawn. Satisfying as many of their mental, emotional, and physical needs as possible reduces difficult behavior. Encouraging the elder to explain what bothers him can reduce an intolerable situation and give the elder a sense of being understood.

Attitude toward death

For some elders, death is simply another transition in the life cycle, marked by peace and even beauty. For others, death is the end of life on earth, the beginning, growth, and ending of which is similar to other growing things. For still others, death is a terrifying void. Whatever their view of death, its approach is a time for review and integration of life's experiences, when a deeper sense of their own contribution to the world takes shape.

Spiritual development

As we age, many of us grow and evolve by shifting our focus from materialism to introspection and a more active search for our inner self. When confronted with serious illness and possible death, everyone seeks a source of strength and inspiration. There is a yearning for a higher purpose—something that transcends everyday materialism.

Thus the interest in holistic medicine, which considers the whole and entire person—body, mind, and spirit. Any physical disease can affect emotions and spirit. Conversely, any emotional or spiritual upset can bring about physiological change. Since the body and mind are components of the physical body, it is futile to treat them separately.

Swiss psychologist Carl Jung believed that humans strive for individuation, balancing our unique experience with our need to be unified with life, mankind, and God. Jungian philosophy says the cycle of life encompasses many opposites. Man's finite consciousness pits these opposites against one another: good-bad, past-future, day-night, joy-sorrow, rich-poor, health-sickness, life-death.

Man's finite state, according to Jung, prefers one over the other, striving for life and rejecting death, for example. But our infinite consciousness transcends opposites. In the same example, man in his infinite consciousness accepts both life and death as part of the perfect whole. When these opposites become integrated, we see a relationship with ourself, with others, with life, and with God.

Another pair of opposites that gives man trouble is past-future. We want to live in the past, or we long for something that has not yet come to pass. We regret the past and worry about the future. We want to be as healthy as we once were, or as young as we once were, or we spend time and energy wishing for some goal beyond our reach. While our energy is spent on the past or the future, we miss the only real life we have: the now.

Opposites create tension and anxiety, but the present is a transcendent state, free of the tensions of opposites. The present is where we find the only true peace and joy.

A third pair of opposites that causes conflict is active-passive. We try actively to run our life, yet sit passively and wait for someone else—a doctor, spouse, child, God—to solve our problems. We resist illness by denying it or fighting it, yet try to cope by passively accepting the situation, with little expectation of change.

Someone trying actively to run his own life will run into insurmountable obstacles. He experiences an awakening, a realization that leads him to seek help, perhaps from something or someone greater than himself. Once free of the opposites, for example, he can be active and passive as the situation requires, without being locked into either extreme.

The antidote to aging

Every elder needs to be valued for himself, but it begins when he values himself. Elders alert and aware of things going on around them are engaged in life. They find new interests, overcome their disabilities, increase their activities.

Fellowship on equal terms becomes an important goal. An elder facing his own mortality has one primary interest: life and living. The search for spirituality and the ability to exchange and share feelings with others replaces the ambition to accumulate wealth and tangible things.

It is important to the elder's psychological and physical health that he have a continuing role in the family and the community. The goal is mutual respect regardless of age. Involvement in community activities may be the answer to loneliness and depression. Talking to a support group, a counselor, or a friend may relieve real aches and pains that spring from inner turmoil.

Every community could profit from association with its elders, who have a wealth of life experiences to share and a new, liberal attitude. They are free of ambition and more interested in people than in power. As society moves forward faster, far too many of our elders are left further behind. Their feelings of powerlessness prevent them from becoming active. What a waste of enormously valuable human resources!

One way to activate our elders is to involve them in school programs. Depending on the elder's interests and abilities, he can visit classrooms and recount his life and experiences. He can read aloud, write poetry, arrange or accompany field trips, stage plays, oversee exercise programs. Responsibility and dignity go together. We must encourage our elders to step forward, take part, and feel alive, despite their disabilities.

Life must balance body, mind, and spirit. But rapid technological development threatens to bring society into imbalance. What is needed is a way for people to re-establish their self-reliance, appreciate such human values as solidarity, and exchange thoughts and dreams. It is the antidote for a world of too much body and too little spirit.

The folk high school experiment

The Netherlands, Denmark, and several other European countries provide the antidote to a too-technical society. Offering subjects like literature, history, art, and community affairs, folk high schools encourage students of all ages to think through new ideas. There are long hours of informal discussion.

All students are equal; there are no wrong answers in folk high school.

The emphasis is on the intellectual and spiritual sides of the students' lives. There is keen recognition that what makes people happy and satisfied with life is not material achievement. Acquiring curiosity and self-respect are the goals in this school, and they are achieved simultaneously by several generations with varying abilities and disabilities.

Folk high schools inspire, organize, encourage, and make sure everybody is involved, in spite of any physical or mental handicaps. I wish I could put a folk high school class in every senior center in the nation!

Judy

It was a second marriage for both of them, a new life at the ages of 55 and 60. They felt young all over again, young and happy and hopeful.

Today Frank has Alzheimer's disease and Judy has Frank's name on a waiting list for a bed in a nursing home. Nothing would please her more than getting the call to bring him in.

"It's more than I can handle," she says. "He's got three grown children that don't care, and I can't do it alone. Even his doctors and psychiatrist agree. He needs 24-hour-a-day care."

But that kind of care is expensive, and Frank wasn't old enough to qualify for Medicare. Until a bed opens up, Judy relies on community services for home care and a few hours of respite on Saturday evenings, when she goes out for dinner with friends.

Three days a week she drives her husband to day care at 9 a.m. and picks him up at 2 p.m. Weekends another day care facility takes him, with transportation arriving at 8:30 a.m. and bringing him home at 1:30 p.m.

While Frank is out, Judy cleans, shops, does her banking. They live on his pension, so money is tight. "And I'm afraid to spend my savings," Judy confesses. "He could live for another 10 years, and I could live another 20."

She describes Frank as "hyper." "He doesn't sleep well. He has to be watched constantly. He'll grab food off the table, or fall and hurt himself. Without his medication he's like a two-year-old," she says.

He's happiest week days at his day care, where the day room is built around a patio. Frank spends hours walking around a tree on the patio, which seems to lull him. By comparison, he needs supervision in order to be outside at his weekend day care, and he is constantly agitated there.

The first signs of the disease came early in the couple's marriage. "We were living back in Michigan then," says Judy, "and we'd drive in the driveway and he'd turn to me and ask, 'Where did we just go?' That happened more than once. And I remember him leaving to go to his sister's house, right in the same town, and he ended up at his other sister's house. She called me to come and get him because he was confused. Confused! In the community he'd lived in for 60 years!"

But those were the aberrations; normally Frank was quite lucid. In fact, they left the north and settled in Arizona soon after their marriage, a decision Frank helped make. Today Judy's dreams of golf and sunsets and time for hobbies have been replaced with appreciation for the number of services available to the aging population in Sun Belt communities. "He's more relaxed, I think, and I find it much easier than it would have been in Michigan," says Judy.

She is president of an Alzheimer's group that raises money for respite care. She attends support groups. She signed up to receive home care for Frank if she becomes ill or disabled.

But she also knows she's on her own until Frank is accepted in a nursing home. She must bathe him, take him to the bathroom, change soiled diapers and rebathe him, *shave him, dress him, and keep him physically safe, sometimes through the night when he won't sleep. The last 18 months have become much more difficult for them both, and Judy knows she's close to reaching her limit.*

"Guilty about putting him in a nursing home?" is her retort when that question comes up. "Absolutely not. What other people think is of no concern to me. I know I can't give Frank the care he's going to need, and I know I've done my best. They make nursing homes for a reason, and a man like Frank is exactly the right reason for a nursing home. I just hope I can do this until I get the call."

CHOOSING HOME HEALTH CARE 5

Y ou cannot prepare for chronic illness. For every elder there comes a time when changing health or a turn of events requires consideration of his living situation. And what family hasn't pondered, "Maybe a nursing home is the answer"?

The answer is not elusive. Five telling predictors of who is most likely to be admitted to a nursing home include:

1. Advanced age

2. Dependency on others for Activities of Daily Living

3. Prior admission to a nursing home

4. Living alone

5. Mental or cognitive problems

Why choose a nursing home?

There are two entry points to a nursing home: from the community and from the hospital. From the hospital, patients are considered for nursing home admission because of end-stage disease or the likelihood of incomplete recovery. In end-stage disease, the elder's medical condition declines until neither rehabilitation nor medical treatment will enable him to return to the community. Incomplete recovery means that more rehabilitation or medical treatment is required in order for the elder to return to the community.

The likelihood of nursing home admission is in direct proportion to the severity and complexity of the elder's illness and the caregiver's inability to meet daily needs. A nursing home may then be the best alternative.

Some elders thrive in nursing homes. The paradox is that the frail, confused, and passive elderly—those most in need of institutional care—are also those who deteriorate and die most rapidly following institutionalization.

The risk is minimized by selecting a nursing home that matches the elder's personal characteristics, and by preparing the elder with information and slow exposure to the new environment.

The elder's primary care physician can help the family decide whether to place their elder in a nursing home. The physician should assess patient and caregiver problems and explore alternative therapies to ensure that other avenues have been considered.

What are the characteristics of a desirable nursing home? Look for an attentive and caring staff, a low turnover rate, an active director of recreational activities, and on-site, progressive physical and occupational therapy departments.

Quality care isn't inexpensive. Only a few long-term services for chronic illness are paid from community, state, or federal funds. Elders and their families usually pay for most nursing home care. Reimbursement is presently available from Medicare and most insurance policies, but only for those suffering critical illness and medical emergencies.

Nursing homes as non-systems

Today's nursing homes more closely resemble chronic disease hospitals for physically and mentally impaired elders. As care centers and homes for ambulatory elders who are no longer self-sufficient, nursing homes leave much to be desired. If a "system" is defined as "a complex unity formed of many diverse parts, subject to a common plan or serving a common purpose," today's nursing homes are by definition non-systems. Nursing homes offer no unity on how to enable an elder to achieve optimum functioning.

But the fact is that at some point some elders can no longer be cared for by the community. Even the best home care arrangement is sometimes not enough.

Muddling through

The nursing home decision may be entirely practical: Maintaining a home and paying others for housekeeping and caregiving may become too expensive. Perhaps the elder himself has had enough of muddling through, coping daily with loneliness and the threat of accidents. Or the decision may be made by the caregiver after long procrastination.

The nursing home decision may be thrust upon the family suddenly, after a debilitating turn in the elder's health or when the caregiver buckles under the strain of constant caregiving, even with the help of outside services. Some families incarcerate older relatives because of the elder's confusion or embarrassing behavior. Some are institutionalized because there is simply no other way to meet their basic social and medical needs.

Just the words "incarcerate" and "institutionalize" reveal our feelings about nursing homes. Considering the origin of the nursing home in the U.S., our attitude is understandable. The nursing home has evolved from a history of charitable care for the helpless. The poorhouse and the large public hospital are its predecessors!

Family members who have chosen to put their elders in nursing homes have been castigated as unfeeling and selfish by analysts and advocates for the elderly. Critics who argue against institutionalization point to the increase in elders residing in long-term care institutions, the greater proportion who die in such institutions, and the well-publicized abuses of the rights and dignity of institutional residents.

But the headlines hardly tell the complete story. The most reliable U.S. national data indicate that almost 80 percent of elder Americans who need long-term care are, in fact, aided wholly or partly by related household members. It is the family that is generally the most reliable source of support for its elders. Statistics show that of the 80 percent of elders who have living children, 75 percent—three out of four!—live in the same household or within 30 miles of those children.

The family remains the primary provider of economic support and informal care for our elders. They care for more elders than do our institutions. And while the average disabled elder residing at home is more independent, and therefore requires less help, than his nursing home counterpart, the needs of homebound elders are still considerable. One-third of elder Americans who receive care at home require constant and prolonged care.

So by some measures, such as the large numbers of residents in nursing homes, families may be accused of abandoning their elders. But by other measures, such as the large numbers of elders living at home through their relatives' assistance, families are doing a good job.

Why choose home health care?

Home care services are appropriate when your elder does not need intensive, full-time institutional care, yet cannot use ambulatory (walk-in) services. The unique value of home care is that it can be tailored to the specific needs of the elder and his family: Appointments are flexible, care is easily altered, and an informal network of family, friends, and volunteers is utilized as much as possible for caregiving.

The differences between institutional living and living at home are obvious, but one word sums them up: choice. As an elder, choosing how you want to live, what you want to do with your days, even how your body feels, is a right of living at home, whether alone or with family. Such choices are rare in institutional life.

Interestingly, the fewer choices we have, regardless of age or health, the fewer decisions and demands we make. Without options and the need to decide, we become docile, undemanding, and removed from life. That might describe the ideal patient if you are trying to manage dozens in an institution, but is it what we want for our elders—or ourselves?

Our elders must be encouraged to speak up, to voice their likes and dislikes and know that what they say is important. When they know their comments are heeded, they will take a more active role in their surroundings. Decision-making keeps them mentally alert, in tune with their bodies and their minds, and aware of the control they have.

Feeling needed and important to the family are priorities for any of us. When an elder comes to live with his child or one spouse tends to another, these elders see their family positions change from carer or equal to dependent. The reaction may be stubborn independence.

The decision to provide home care involves practical, financial, and emotional factors. The family's priorities have to be evaluated. Is the elder's care the paramount concern? Or do the needs of children/grandchildren take precedence, with the family relying on whatever energy, affection, and money are left over for the patient? Who will be the caregiver? Is a hospital or medical center accessible in an emergency? Is there a source of nurses and other health care professionals? What about routine supplies and facilities for laboratory testing and other technical procedures? And, almost as important as accessible medical care, is respite available for a tired caregiver?

You must realistically evaluate the energy and time available from family and friends. If family members are the chief caregivers, their employment, health, and other daily responsibilities must be considered. If there is more than one family member, rotation of responsibilities can usually be worked out. If one person is the main caregiver, he or she must be allotted sufficient time for his or her own physical and mental well-being.

The ideal atmosphere

Under ideal circumstances, those who love and understand the elder can best restore his emotional balance, build trust and hope, and stimulate the elder to mobilize all his resources to cope with stress and cooperate in rehabilitation. Those family members closest to the elder can best anticipate his interests and needs and provide resources that will be stimulating and gratifying.

The elder who is supported by the family's love, respect, and stimulation thrives. The more everyday activities he can carry on, the more "like himself" he will feel and become. And aside from having the resources for the elder's favorite activities and interests, home is where his pace can be respected: He need not be pushed to go faster nor wait unduly, nor have pleasures terminated arbitrarily to fit some rigid schedule, nor be awakened at the convenience of staff. The home schedule can be adjusted to the elder's desires and needs.

This is no easy task, particularly for a family caregiver who has her own health problems or other family demands. But even as the elder becomes more disabled or a family caregiver suffers burnout, there are options, outside resources, and answers that can extend the elder's stay in the community.

Working out a plan for home care can seem complicated and overwhelming to both the patient and the family. The goal is to create an environment that is comforting to the patient and workable for all concerned.

Statistically, the person most likely to use home care services is a female over 65 who exhibits several chronic health problems but can cope with her Activities of Daily Living with minimal help.

I advocate observing three principles in developing a policy for the care of elders at home:

1. Start with an assessment of the resources the elder has, not what he lacks.

2. Emphasize continuity. The passage into old age should not be a radical departure from his previous lifestyle.

3. Finally, the elder must have a say in every decision concerning his life.

In any assessment of an elder's health situation, the first step is gathering all the data and then reading between the lines, taking stock of what goes on when different problems interact with one another. The next step is organizing the data so both the elder and the caregiver can identify all available options and be familiar with those that seem most plausible. But the most important step is the first: to understand and clarify the basic situation. Don't pull any punches here; this is the time for brutal honesty and unblinking examination. Insight is essential to decision-making.

Whenever possible, decisions must be made by the family and the elder. The decision for home care must, of course, be fully supported by the potential primary family caregiver. Unless the patient is too confused or disoriented, he is included in the discussion and should contribute as much as possible to the planning process.

Once the situation has been evaluated, the caregiver family can explore the issues they've identified. Are the elder's problems emotional, physical, social, or simply consequences of aging? When problems are detangled and handled individually, what seems overwhelming is no longer such a formidable problem. Once any initial panic is allayed by an understanding of the problem, a rewarding solution is likely to fall into place. For example, it may be important to understand the elder's distress about aging in order for the family to accept his reaction and deal with the elder from a new perspective.

The principles of home care

There are three levels of home care, corresponding to three levels of elder dysfunction:

1. **Intensive home care** for the patient who needs multiple medical and nursing care services.

2. **Intermediate/rehabilitative home care** for the patient who needs nursing supervision and direct care, such as physical therapy, but who is otherwise stable.

3. **Basic/minimal home care** for the patient who needs maintenance care—such as personal or supportive service—but who is medically stable.

There are also three essential goals of any home care plan:

1. **To enable** the elder to stay healthy and functionally independent as long as possible

2. **To provide** access to good:

   • short-term recuperative, rehabilitative, and preventive services

   • long-term services to manage serious chronic disease and disability

   • support services when disease is terminal

3. **To encourage** as much patient autonomy and responsibility as possible

Whether it is a sudden, catastrophic illness or severe chronic illness, the principles of caregiving should consider the whole person, not just the symptoms. Home care should:

- Make life worth living

- Decrease isolation

- Maximize the elder's available resources

- Balance the familiar with the new

- Be flexible yet consistent

- Do things to, for, and with the elder. In other words, involve.

Even a medically stable elder may require top-flight home nursing skills. If an elder has been hospitalized, for example, he may have a residue of difficult emotions: disorientation, confusion, a shattered self-image, anger at perceived or actual mistakes, anxiety about continuing painful treatments, despair for the future, as well as weakness and decreased control. A nursing home may or may not be sensitive to these emotions. Family most certainly is.

Caregivers must also recognize the cognitive and emotional changes that occur as a relative ages. There is often anger and depression due to real or perceived loss of control over one's body and mind. Adjustments to new routines, environments, and people can be confusing and stressful. Role changes usually accompany disability. Self-esteem and self-identity are threatened whenever one's body requires physical rehabilitation.

Sometimes communication and reassurance are all that is needed: Once the elder expresses his feelings to someone who validates them, he is relieved.

Illness creates disruptions in the usual family routines, and may change individual roles and expectations. In most instances the family caregiver provides much of the daily support. She is the one who must deal with the patient's moods, any sudden behavior changes, and the altered status of family members.

The objective of home care is to keep the home life as normal as possible for the elder and others in the house, and at the same time provide quality medical care. Whatever the illness and whether the elder is at home, in a nursing home, or in a hospital, both the elder's and the family's physical and emotional resources will be taxed. Eldercare can change the pattern of family life.

Allowing the elder to maintain a sense of dignity is vital. He should be invited to join everything he can take part in. What he needs is to feel part of the family, part of society.

But caregivers must remember that respect for the elder's dignity also includes respect for the elder's limits. The elder should be encouraged to do as much as possible without attempting the impossible. Many caretakers feel that because they are in charge, they know what the patient needs and should have. Let the elder express his needs. Let the elder do everything possible for himself.

If the elder is encouraged each day to do a little more, both his strength and independence will increase. It is impossible to predict how much progress a patient can make. Evaluate every possibility for independent effort by the elder. When being bathed, what areas of his body can he do himself? Encourage him to initiate and carry out his own exercises. Active exercise, when allowed, is more effective than passive efforts performed by a caregiver.

Your elder should:

- Be as independent as possible

- Participate in as many activities as age, injury, or illness allow

- Perform simple tasks like bathing, dressing, shaving, shampooing, and light housekeeping

- Act sensibly during recovery, following prescribed treatments and medications

Attending to ADLs

Many health conditions affect the elder's ability to attend to personal grooming, eating, walking, moving around in bed, bathing, and other Activities of Daily Living. Elders should undergo regular ADL tests to determine their limitations and detect changes in their ability to perform self-care. Specific activities have been designed for the elder who needs reminding, remotivating, or retraining to help him perform ADLs.

When an elder requires ADL help, his caregiver must keep these three points in mind:

1. Good balance is needed to perform independent self care.

2. Any self-care activity is made up of many steps, and sometimes the elder must conquer these steps one by one.

3. The elder needs the caregiver's patience and encouragement.

To the third point I would add six more tips:

1. Use the same simple, clear, brief phrases every day to instruct and encourage the elder.

2. Don't rush him. Allow him time to complete an activity at his own pace.

3. Find out if he prefers certain activities. Concentrate on those activities until he masters them.

4. Give him ADL training at the same time that he would normally do that task.

5. Allow him to do as much as he can for himself.

6. Help him to use and master any adaptive equipment ordered for him. See that his equipment is in good working order and positioned for easy access.

Patient care must include recreation adapted to his interests and abilities. Does your elder's routine allow him to watch his favorite television shows? Has he always been a jigsaw puzzle solver or a bird watcher? Did he play cards every Tuesday with a group of friends for more than a decade? What similar activities can he do now, and how can he progress to the point of returning to a favorite activity? Every elder should have work to do that carries over from one day to the next, have opportunities to learn, and have a social and recreational life to enjoy.

I think of the word "recreation" as re-creation—to begin anew. But in practice, recreation is more than a new beginning. It can turn the mind away from pressures and worries and toward satisfaction. Recreation relaxes the mind and so relaxes the body. Recreation is as important as medication and therapy to recovery and adjustment.

"Remotivation" is the process of renewing a patient's will to live. It stimulates his desire to be active and to learn. "Resocialization" is the process of renewing a patient's awareness of others. It stimulates his desire and ability to participate in groups. All are necessary on a daily basis.

Home health care is hard work, but for the family determined to care for its elder at home, the rewards can far outweigh the problems. The pattern of home care will depend on the condition and needs of the elder, the participation of other family members, and the financial resources available.

I believe home care will flourish because it is ethically, financially, medically, socially, and morally correct. Its time has come. It works—not because of technology, but because of people!

Alicia

"You're the eyes and the ears of the doctor," says Alicia Anatelli, a home health nurse for two years. "Sure, you keep in touch with the others on the team—I fill out a communication sheet at every home visit. The occupational therapist, the speech therapist, your supervisor all know what's going on. The social worker arranges transportation and Meals on Wheels. But the home health nurse is considered the case manager.

"When you go into someone's home, you can't help but get to know them. It's different than being a hospital nurse. You become part of the family, and they want to know your family, too. When college coaches were recruiting my son for football, my patients wanted daily reports. I may be in their home every day at the start of a case, then five times a week, then four, then three. Sometimes I'm the only person some of these people talk to all day.

"So it's more than just checking vital signs. Typically I will change the dressing on a wound, listen to lung and heart sounds, check for edema—that's swelling—ask how they're eating, make sure the bowels are moving. Things like that.

"The way I see it, I'm preventing a lot of complications. If I notice weight gain and the lungs filling up with fluid, I talk to the doctor and get a diuretic prescribed. Things like that are what keep these people out of the hospital.

"Here's an example: The patient was released after open heart surgery. He needed someone to see that the wounds healed; observe the catheter; assess his lungs,

urine, and blood pressure. And he needed a support
assessment. His wife was with him, and she learned things
to watch for. But they needed an aide to come in and
bathe him daily, and a physical therapist got him walking,
got him stronger. The wife couldn't have handled all this
alone. But with home care, in 10 weeks he was discharged
to his own care and regular doctor visits.

"What gets difficult? I guess chest pains, for exam-
ple, because we have no portable EKG or portable oxy-
gen. In cases like that I have to call 911. The only other
drawback for a home health nurse is that you're by your-
self. You've got to be sure of your own assessment. When I
worked in a hospital, we'd always be running cases by
one another. In home care, there's no back-up. You gotta
be good.

"That's why I do it," Alicia Anatelli smiles.

Dr. Arnold S. Goldstein *is a nationally known tax and asset protection specialist.*

As an attorney, professor and author of over 100 books on finance and law, his tax-resolution strategies have helped thousands of individuals and businesses solve their tax problems. He has been featured on hundreds of radio and TV shows and in numerous magazines. His firm, Arnold S. Goldstein & Associates, P.A., represents clients nationwide.

He is a graduate of Northwestern University (B.S., 1961) and Suffork University (MBA, 1966 and LL.M., 1975). He also holds a law degree from the New England School of Law (J.D., 1964) and a doctorate from Northeastern University (Ph.D. in business and economic policy, 1990). He is a member of the Massachusetts and Federal Bar and numerous professional, academic and civic organizations.

THE NEXT BEST PLACE TO HOME

6

No place is like home, a comfortable, familiar surrounding where a person has lived for many years. It is filled with precious memories and offers personality, comfort and security, especially to the elderly. But circumstances may create a need which cannot be filled even with home care; and, to receive the type of help or care he or she needs, a facility other than a nursing home may be sufficient. This is usually an Assisted Living Facility.

But, wherever the move may be, there will be a drastic change in lifestyle. This can be equally traumatic to the individual as well as the family.

The caregiver or family member(s) must make, or assist with this most important decision. They may experience guilt, anger, frustration, or loss; emotions eased by speaking with trained counselors, spiritual advisors, and others who have had similar experiences. Their guidance should help make the move easier.

Where an elderly person goes will depend on several factors; most notably their health and their wealth. The patient should be involved in as much of the decision-making procedure as possible. Informed patients and families make the best decisions. Get professional advice from a social worker, hospital discharge planner, and financial asset protection specialist. They can provide you with invaluable information. Visiting and comparing different facilities is the only way to see what is available in alternative living.

Know Assisted Living

Know your own needs and your loved one's. It is a prerequisite to a proper decision. Consider:

- Are you/your loved one ambulatory?

- Do you/your loved one have cognitive impairments?

- Do you want or can you have independence?

- What are your special needs and considerations - diet, supervision, etc? Talk to the faculty dietician or food supervisor. Make them aware of your particular needs.

- What kind of facility and services best fills those needs?

- Do you want a private or shared room?

- How will you pay; cash, private insurance, Medicaid, Supplemental Security Income? If paying privately what can you/your loved one afford?

Most importantly, check these essential points:

- Does the facility offer cost effective quality care?

- Foster resident's independence?

- Treat each resident with dignity and respect?

- Promote the individuality of each resident?

- Allow each resident choice of care and lifestyle?

- Protect each resident's privacy?

- Involve family and friends in care planning?

- Provide a safe, residential environment?

- Make the assisted living residence a valuable community asset?

> Always interview the administrator. Let them explain their policies and services and answer any questions you may have.

> Astute assisted living operators want their residents to have as much control over their lives as they desire.

> Assisted living facilities are filling the gap between independent living and nursing home care.

> Assisted living is an example of the good news in aging. With it's growing popularity and lower costs, it is easy to see that assisted living facilities are a product whose time has come.

Financing Assisted Living

Once you have chosen a residence for yourself or loved one, you generally will meet with the administrator, once again, for the pre-admission appraisal. The facility staff will assess you/your loved one's physical capabilities, mental condition and social service needs. You may be asked to provide a complete physician's evaluation form. Is there a written care plan for each resident?

Are resident's needs addressed periodically? Does this process include the resident, their family and facility staff and resident's physician?

When may a contract be terminated? What are the removal, discharge and refund policies?

What restrictions and other liabilities exist?

Do fees include accommodations, personal care, health care and supportive services? Are additional services available if needed?

Are billing and credit policies fair?

Must residents purchase renters' insurance for personal property in their units?

Does the home accept Supplemental Security Income residents?

Before finalizing an admissions agreement, inquire about complaints, or legal action taken against that facility. In every state, the Long-Term Care Ombudsman is an advocate for facility residents, and investigates complaints and helps resolve resident problems.

The Type of Alternative Lifestyle facilities

There are several distinct types of facilities and before you begin the search, you should know the type of facility that is most appropriate for you.

Retirement Homes/Continuing Care Facilities are individual apartments or single rooms in a multi-unit building exclusively designed for older persons. They offer many support services, such as meals, transportation, housekeeping, laundry, and social and recreational programs. Most allow home health care companions, or provide such services as required. Senior living communities can be rental, condo, or a life care arrangement.

Generally, they are usually not covered by most long-term care insurance policies.

Residential Living Facilities

(RLFs) are for people who cannot live alone; but who do not need skilled nursing services. Their residents are independent and require only minimal supervision. However, RLFs also are appropriate for even moderately confused people with few or no other medical needs. Some RLFs specialize in aged, persons with Alzheimer's disease, younger cognitive impaired individuals.

These homes, usually in residential neighborhoods, have been modified for about six residents. Most features gardens or yards, living or family rooms, and a common dining room. These homes provide social interaction and recreational and social activities.

RLFs are staffed 24-hours a day, for emergencies and to supervise the physical or cognitive impaired. They can assist with bedside care, personal hygiene, grooming, dressing, meals and other daily activities. Some RLFs for an additional fee, include transportation to shopping centers or other outings, cable TV, newspaper delivery or religious activities.

RLFs are usually least expensive but are not covered by Medicaid, because they do not offer medical services. In some cases, SSI payments can reimburse the facility.

RLFs are state licensed, and subject to regulation for admissions, theft and loss policies, and evictions. They are also periodically inspected by the Department of Social Services.

An alternative care facility provides on-going care and related services to a minimum of five residents in one location. They may be freestanding or part of a larger life-care community facility, such as an Adult Congregate Living Facility. They generally do not have individual residences or independent living units.

Their facilities are not a long-term care facility, nursing home, hospital or clinic, boarding home, rest home, home for the aged, a place that provides domiciliary, residential, or retirement care, or, a hospice. Nor do they treat Alcoholics, or drug addicts; or the mentally ill.

Alternative Facility Provider, provides 24-hour care and service, sufficient to support Activities of Daily Living (ADLS), or Cognitive Impairment. They provide all meals and accommodate special dietary needs. A staff is in the facility at all times, to support the needs of residents and to manage all medical emergencies and medical needs, including the services of a physician or nurse, and the administration of drugs.

Assisted Living Facilities (ALFs) are the fastest growing type of residential housing for senior citizens providing "upscale" living, they fill a void in the care of older Americans who cannot live at home, or who need extra support; but not necessarily nursing-care. These maintenance-free residences promote maximum independence for older persons.

Residents share community living and dining areas; and participate together in social and recreational activities. They combine independence with personal care, in a warm community setting. It thus combines housing, personalized supportive services, and health care, customized to individuals needing help with daily living activities. (ADLs).

Nearly 8 million senior citizens need assistance with daily living activities and this number will double by 2020. Over one million Americans now live in about 20,000 assisted living communities. Residents can be affluent or low income, disabled, or suffering from Alzheimer's disease or Parkinson and need help with mobility.

Many Assisted Living residences compare to up-scale hotels. Most have 25 to 120 units, varying from a single room or couple-shared dwellings to full apartments.

ALFs can be free-standing, independent retirement communities; part of a continuing care community; or campus-like settings, affiliated with a nursing home. They are frequently tied-in with community support services, and may be operated by profit or not-for-profit companies.

Assisted Living Facilities combine safety concerns, personalized special support services and health care, tailored to those requiring assistance with activities of daily living (ADLs). Services while similar to RLF they are generally more expensive. By providing many services available in a skilled nursing facility, through the strategic alliances on an as-needed basis with home health agencies and other outside professionals, ALFs are an alternative for residents who do not need intensive medical care or a more costly nursing home.

ALFs fall into three categories:

The Hospitality model provides hotel-like services, and are for healthy residents with minimal service needs.

The Personal Care model provides personal care assistance for frail residents or where the well spouse and the impaired spouse wish to live together with on-site support services.

The Aging-in-place model has on-site care for chronic conditions and can provide some skilled nursing services and accommodate the residents needs.

There is no standard definition for "assisted living", and facilities are regulated differently between states and vary in the services and level or care they provide.

Most Assisted living facilities typically provide: Staff to meet scheduled and unscheduled needs; emergency calls; personal care assistance (dressing, grooming, eating, bathing, toileting, walking and other Activities of Daily Living (ADLs); meals; housekeeping and laundry services; utilities; health promotion and exercise, transportation and ambulance services. Assistance with medications, according to state regulations are in each community listing page as "supervision, administration, or monitoring" Long term; Assisted living Facilities provide increasing levels of care as the resident grows more frail.

Monthly costs vary based upon location, unit size, and services required by the resident. Most assisted living residences charge monthly rates, but some require long-term contracts. The rate may cover all services or with supplemental charges for special services. Obtain an itemized list of services agreed upon, and the cost of additional or optional services.

Assisted living can be prohibitively expensive. Most Assisted Living Communities accept private pay, only. Some state and local governments subsidize rent or services for the income-eligible, others subsidize residents with Supplemental Security Income (SSI) or Medicaid. Some states have Medicaid waiver programs to pay for assisted living. Medicaid does not reimburse for assisted living, since the services are not considered medical. Many residences have their own financial assistance programs.

Depending on all individuals' health insurance programs, certain costs may be reimbursable. More liberal policies will include the nursing home benefit portion of the policy for 'alternative care' or through 'an alternative place' of care benefit.

For More Information Contact:

Caregiver Resource Centers (CRCs); churches and temples; residential care home referral services; senior centers; senior information and referral (I&R) programs; Area Agencies on Aging (AAAs); doctors and other health professionals; case managers; hospital social workers and discharge planners; long-term Care Ombudsman, libraries; the local or state Department of Health Services or Department of Aging. Additional information about ALFS can be found though the Continuing Care Accreditation Commission in Washington DC; and. Assisted Living Federation of America (ALFA). Assisted Living Facilities are listed with the Assisted Living Facilities Association of America.

How to find an Assisted Living Residence:

Call the national Eldercare locator service at (800) 677-1116, 9am - 5pm Monday-Friday. Contact you local area agency on aging, generally listed in the blue pages of your telephone directory. Check your library for directories of retirement facilities. Call ALFA for a listing or residences in your state at (703) 691-8100; or, visit their web-site at www.alfa.org.

Financial Services agencies offer general financial information to seniors, and/or help seniors with tax issues.

But...if you need a nursing home...

While every caring family wants their loved one in a home environment, the reality is that is not always possible.

Hopefully, before you decide to put someone in a nursing home, you will explore the wide range of alternative services. Although this book is pro-home health care, it is not anti-Nursing home.

A well-educated consumer is a smart consumer. And, choosing a Nursing Home is a very important decision. If possible, research you options at least three months prior to anticipated placement.

The assisted living facility checklist includes many of the same points for an appropriate nursing home. Of course, some options do not apply; and there are additional considerations with the nursing home that will best accommodate the patient. But use the ALF checklist as a guide, to create you own nursing home checklist.

If you understand how a nursing home operates, you can more wisely plan ahead. Have the patient evaluated by the appropriate state or local authorities to determine the level of care required. This is necessary to prevent the facility from 'dumping' an individual who does not meet the qualifications of the home's level of care. There are basically two levels of nursing homes and they fill different needs.

1. **Intermediate Nursing Home** care are for long-term disabilities or stabilized Illnesses. They aid with basic daily living needs. In most cases, medication is dispensed by a RN or LPN. They keep residents functioning at their optimum level through rehabilitation services.

2. **A Skilled Nursing Home** is usually for short-term residents, where the goal of rehabilitation to return to long-term, or, make the facility their home. Patients get continuous care and personal assistance by nurse aids, RNs

and LPNs (both of which dispense medications under a physicians supervision), Staff includes restorative, physical, occupational, speech and sometimes respiratory therapists; as well as social workers, and an activities department

Medicaid Planning and Protecting your wealth from Nursing Home Costs

Today, over 30 million Americans are over 65, only a century ago, fewer than 3% of all Americans could hope to reach that age.

We are truly seeing the graying of America, and it is presenting dangers to our wealth - the realization that we may lose our wealth for long-term care and other geriatric health costs.

Consider just a few eye opening statistics.

Life expectancy at birth is now 80.

- If you and your spouse reach age 65, the chances are excellent that you will reach 90.

- The over-85 seniors are the fastest growing age group

There are of course, many reasons for this. People no longer commonly die early from communicable diseases. We now increasingly die from heart disease and cancer, diseases more related to our environment, heredity and lifestyle. Whatever the reasons, we will live longer with each successive generation.

I have many clients who have managed to keep their assets intact during their working years. They not only looked forward to a financially secure retirement, but also making their children's life a bit easier through a sizeable inheritance.

But it doesn't always go according to plan.

One couple who I have represented for years illustrates the point. Charles and Clara managed to accumulate about a half a million for their retirement; more than enough to see themselves through their golden years while leaving money to their two now middle-aged children. But Clara's vision of a happy secure retirement soon vanished when Charles developed Parkinson's disease and spent eight years in a nursing home. In eight years the couple lost nearly every asset they owned, leaving Clara to live out her life on a dismal social security check. Clara would quickly remind you "when you are still relatively young and in good health, you don't think about old age health problems, nursing homes and the thought that your money will go to cover these costs.

But we do grow old which certainly beats the alternative. And not all of us will die peacefully in our sleep at home. For many within the graying generation their final years will be in nursing homes, and when it happens their wealth can vanish even quicker than their health. That is why it is so important to have Long Term Care Insurance.

Why you must protect against long term costs

What are the odds that you or your spouse will end up in a nursing home?

What are the odds that your parents will end up in a nursing home?

Quite good!

Seven out of ten couples over 65 will see at least one spouse in a nursing home.

- About two-thirds of the men and over half the women over 65 will need at least some nursing home care.

- A decent nursing home costs about $60,000 a year - but their costs are skyrocketing and may double within 10 years.

- Over half the people who go into a nursing home become impoverished after only four months.

- Three out of four nursing home patients are women because four out of five wives outlive their husbands.

Paying for Long-Term Care

So, how can you protect your wealth against these almost predictable costs - perhaps the last but greatest danger to your wealth; other than estate taxes?

You can forget help from the government. Medicare does not pay for nursing home costs, except for a brief stay in skilled care facilities after hospitalization. But fewer than 2% of all nursing home patients fall within this category. Nor should you expect the government to expand its nursing home coverage under medicare. This is one expense Uncle Sam expects you to pay yourself - until you are impoverished and can no longer afford it. Only then will Medicaid cover your costs - after most of your assets are consumed.

Nor will your private medical insurance or HMO cover you. They simply don't consider long-term care as "medical" care.

Of course, if you're wealthy and can afford upwards of $50,000 annually for a nursing home, Long Term Care costs are of little consequence to you. For those who have less than $25,000 in assets and very sick Medicaid or Medical welfare will cover the costs of long term care.

The Home Care and Nursing Home Insurance Solution

This is your one best solution to a thorny problem.

I know. I bought a policy when I was 55. No, it's not money I like to spend, but it at least spares me the anguish of making bad choices if my wife or myself should ever need a nursing home.

If you are to buy nursing home insurance, do it when you are younger. A 50 year old, for instance, pays about half the total payments of a 75 year-old and he has many more years of coverage. Moreover, you will more easily qualify for coverage when you are younger and healthier.

Many Americans are coming to the realization, they would prefer to spend tens of thousands on insurance rather than hundreds of thousands on nursing homes. For them it is a smart way to preserve their wealth, to maintain their financial security, and to retain their dignity by remaining self-sufficient rather than a burden.

That's why Americans are planning ahead to protect themselves in advance. The most popular solution is long term care insurance covering nurses, at-home helpers and companies, assisted living homes and skilled nursing homes.

Under a long -term care policy, you receive a daily benefit to cover the cost of a nursing home stay or skilled or custodial care in your home. Generally, your benefits are paid when you are unable to handle the normal activities of daily living.

Long term care insurance covers a person against the costs of home health care, community-based care (assisted living, etc.) and of course nursing home care.

Long-term care insurance gives you sound financial protection, and is a valuable tool to help you protect your nest egg and your family from substantial medical costs.

The annual long term care insurance premium investment is often less than the actual cost of just one-month in a care situation. Long-term care insurance may make good financial sense for you. Recent industry articles indicate that long-term care insurance is such a valuable planning tool that financial advisors may face legal action if they neglect to at least recommend consideration of this type coverage.

If you are like most people, you have been saving for the future and planning your retirement. Unfortunately, people often overlook the need to protect against the expense associate with a prolonged illness that requires special care. Although it is difficult to think about, the fact is that more than 40% of all people over the age of 65 will enter a nursing home during their lifetime. And many more will be there for YEARS.

Therefore it is smart to plan ahead and be prepared. In this day and age, few can deny the wisdom of owning long term care insurance protection to assure a carefree retirement. Few want to spend down assets prematurely for unexpected, prolonged care. Few people want to be a burden to their family.

BUILDING A HOME CARE TEAM 7

All home-based services have one aim—to help the elder live at home in safe, comfortable, clean surroundings, with access to food and health care. Home care allows an elder to stay at home during the course of his illness. Home care gives an elder control by promoting dignity, self-care, and individuality.

Home care is a team effort to maximize the strengths of the patient while minimizing his weaknesses. The professional part of that care may come from one or more organizations: government-sponsored agencies, nonprofit agencies, private agencies, and/or hospital-based programs.

Home care is usually provided in the elder's own home or the home of family. It can consist of a few hours a week of friendly volunteer visitors, transportation to a senior center for a hot midday meal, and occasional handyman help around the house. Or it can be 24-hour-a-day skilled nursing care.

Many communities offer an impressive array of home assistance, both private and public. Payment is usually out-of-pocket or through government assistance entitlement plans if the patient or family qualifies.

A community referral service will help orient the family of an elder. It can provide information on housing, day care, education, emergency response programs, entitlement programs, legal services, health care, health insurance, nutrition, recreation, respite, taxes, transportation, help with government forms, and emergency crisis counseling.

There are several home care styles to consider:

- Family and friends may keep in touch with an elder who is staying in his home with the aid of home health professionals and other support services.

- A family caregiver may move the elder into her home and rely on community services.

- The family may investigate semi-independent living arrangements that provide modest assistance for residents, such as meal programs, health care, and social activities.

- Family members may design a unique home care program that suits their elder and their lifestyle.

Whatever your home care style, all home care programs consist of three stages. The first is a consideration of whether home care is appropriate for the elder and his family. If the answer is yes, the second stage is setting a plan to attain goals and teaching the patient and family the necessary skills and routines. (If the answer is no, that doesn't rule out the possibility that when the elder's status has changed, home care may again be considered.) The third stage takes place at home, where the elder and the family put into action the techniques learned.

The non-family component of home care is physician-directed and nurse-coordinated. The team works as a unit under the day-to-day direction of the rehabilitation nurse, but responsibility for the elder is shared by the entire team. It shifts between members depending on the elder's needs. The non-family members may be professionals, paraprofessionals, and/or volunteers. Some may visit the home daily, some five times a week, some only as needed.

The home care team may include:

> The elder
>
> The family
>
> Physician
>
> Medical social worker
>
> Registered nurse
>
> Licensed vocational nurse
>
> Physical, speech, and/or occupational therapist
>
> Dietitian
>
> Counselors
>
> Health care aides
>
> Adult day care workers
>
> Handy/chore people
>
> Homemakers
>
> Bath attendants
>
> Companions
>
> Volunteer visitors
>
> Meal deliverers
>
> Drivers

Notice who is at the top of the list. The elder is the most important member of the team. All team efforts, decisions, and support must benefit the elder.

In the home setting there is no "You must." The approach is, instead, "You might"—presenting options and strategies to the elder. He participates in every aspect of his care. Other members can bring only their expertise, their care, their concern, and their efforts.

Just as essential to the team is the family, as caregivers and as kin, plain and simple, with all the connotations of family values. The effectiveness of the family in this role is highly dependent upon how close a relationship they establish with the rest of the team and the elder.

If a number of services must be coordinated for the elder's well being, a specific plan of care is usually designed by a physician or medical social worker in concert with the team that will implement the plan. Because the patient's multifaceted problems—medical, psychological, and financial—are ordinarily beyond the capacity of any one individual, a system of communication and regular meetings assists in developing goals, discussing treatment plans, and assessing progress or regression.

Often, one goal is to prepare the elder and the caregiver for the eventual absence of the rest of the team. If cure or full recovery is not possible, the team must focus on teaching and shoring up the abilities of the caregiver while easing the elder's downhill course.

Because they are aware of the elder's living environment, the team can set goals accurately. When goals are reviewed, it is often with the team sitting together in the home, where the family and the elder feel confident to add their input. Not infrequently, lay assessments are right on target. It is a humbling experience when home care professionals realize they are not the only ones with insight into the rehabilitation process.

Each team member has separate and distinct functions that must be fine-tuned and coordinated. Each is an individual, with the usual ego and desire for recognition and distinction. Nevertheless, the group must combine its skills to produce a synergistic program that is greater than the sum of its parts. This is the hallmark of a good interdisciplinary team.

Unlike a multidisciplinary team, where individuals from several disciplines establish their own goals, an interdisciplinary team works toward common goals. The interdisciplinary team is the ideal in home health care.

Flexibility is important. The home health care team must be able to adapt to changing situations to meet the elder's changing moods and needs. Routine must be secondary to the support of the elder as an individual, not merely a sick body. On the other hand, consistency is important so the patient knows what he can count on. To maintain equilibrium, comfort, and morale, the home health care team must make alleviation of pain and consistency of care its priorities.

What should you look for in your home care team?

1. They are advisors to patient care planning and development.

2. They may experience role-blurring or cross-training. For example, a home health aide may perform exercises prescribed by both the physical and occupational therapists.

3. Services are frequently provided in concentrated periods. For example, the nurse may assist the elder and perform complex dressing care while the social worker counsels the caregiver in use of community resources and ways to facilitate the elder's self-care.

4. Services are delivered according to the elder's needs and preferences rather than rigid hospital schedules.

5. The elder and caregiver are involved in the planning and care because the professional members are not always available.

6. The physician relies on the assessment and evaluation reports of nurses and therapists to determine changes in treatment.

7. A nurse/case manager, working with the elder, coordinates the planning and delivery of services.

8. The team teaches the elder and caregiver to recognize early signs of deterioration or undesirable effects to be reported to the physician.

9. The team formulates and drills the elder and caregiver on the plan in the event of emergencies such as drug reactions, falls, etc.

Coordinating services is key

Continuity of care is critical in home care, especially if the patient is among the frail elderly, who are especially vulnerable to poorly coordinated care. The care received in an acute hospital must be linked with the care in the nursing home, rehabilitation program, office practice, day care center, respite program, other community-based programs, and the home. The coordination of these numerous providers is no less important than the medical attention the elder receives.

Sometimes the elders at the highest risk and with the highest priority for home care programs are the ones least likely to receive it. These include the recently bereaved, those living alone, elders with mental disorders, and the old-old.

Disconnected from a social network of services, they are too often ignored or passed over by traditional programs.

Fortunately, alternate sources are available and new ones are constantly emerging. Whether funding is available, whether waiting lists are reasonable, and whether fees are manageable are questions without easy answers. But resources for answers are also constantly emerging

One is the National Rehabilitation Information Center (NARIC). NARIC is probably the largest source of information on disability-related research, supportive services, and consumer products. REHABDATA is a computerized database of disability-related documents. ABLEDATA is a computerized list of thousands of commercially available products appropriate for elders and those with disabilities.

Local Area Agencies on Aging are clearinghouses of information on elder programs. Their purpose is to marshal and arrange services for elders from the resources in the community. The quality and usefulness of any Area Agency on Aging depends on the vagaries of local budget and staffing constraints. You can find the phone number of the closest AAA in the yellow pages under social service organizations, guide to human services, or aging services.

Caring from afar

Families that live many miles from their elder face unique

problems, including the guilt of not being able to help with the day-to-day difficulties or a crisis. It takes time, personal visits and, usually, money to line up the assistance needed for long-distance eldercare.

A good start is with a telephone directory of the elder's community so the family can network community programs from afar. A directory also makes it easier to contact the elder's friends and neighbors. Ask for specific help from people within the support system. Make sure you have a back-up system in the event of an emergency. And give key people within the support system the names of other key people to contact.

Call the Office for Aging in your elder's state capital and ask for the number of the local Area Agency on Aging. The AAA should be able to provide free booklets on eldercare, a directory of local services, and access to free care managers who will visit your elder, assess health and homemaking needs, and suggest additional services.

Numerous materials are available to health care professionals, elders, and their families regarding products, equipment, financial assistance, travel, leisure, activities, public policy, legislation, and educational and vocational opportunities. Most large cities publish a guide to community resources, which should be a standard reference in all home health agencies.

State and local chapters of organizations like the Arthritis Foundation, American Heart Association, American Cancer Society, and National Head Injury Foundation can supply valuable free information related to specific disabilities. For a free Caregiver Resource Kit write to:

The American Association of Retired Persons
AARP Fulfillment, EE0926
601 E Street NW
Washington DC 20049

Private care managers

Geriatric care management helps those who live far from their elder or work at full-time jobs. A geriatric care manager finds and coordinates short- and long-term services. He or she may be a social worker, nurse, psychologist, or someone with a degree in a nonmedical aspect of gerontology. Private care managers set up private practices to counsel and assist families planning long-term eldercare. Fees vary by assignment.

Care managers will help with details, plan, and research. For additional fees they take on the entire job of consulting and supervising the elder's long-term care, including arranging for community-based services, recommending nursing homes, and attending to financial arrangements. At this level, the manager becomes a surrogate in the burdensome job that families have traditionally—and by necessity—assumed for their elders. Like other professionals, care managers will consult with the family for an hour or two or take over whatever extent of the work the family cannot do.

Finding a good private care manager saves time and energy. Your stress level will be reduced and you will rest easier knowing your elder is well cared for.

If a private care manager is not practical, consider other service coordinators. More than a third of the Area Agencies on Aging offer case management or service coordination, as well as the federally mandated services (home-delivered meals, free transportation, illness prevention programs, etc.) and referrals to other services. Another resource:

> National Association of Private Geriatric Care Managers
> Tucson, AZ

For the names of private geriatric care managers in your state, send $2 and a self-addressed stamped envelope to:

> Children of Aging Parents
> Woodbourne Office Campus, Suite 302A
> 1609 Woodbourne Rd.
> Levittown, PA 19057

The physician as home care director

Physicians have a reason and a responsibility to participate in home care. The chronically disabled, the frail and dependent, and the terminally ill are patients whose quality of life often can be improved by home care without compromising their medical status. When enhanced quality of life and patient and family preference are added to decreased cost and lower incidence of medical complications, home care clearly becomes the new community standard of care for certain health problems.

Active physician involvement and leadership are mandatory if home care is to reach its full potential, especially in providing optimal care to elders living in the community.

No aspect of medical practice has experienced greater change over the past 50 years than that of physicians in home health care. The home is an unusual place to practice medicine, and the demands on the physician are unique. He or she must step out of the high-tech world of medicine and into a foreign environment.

The first time the physician enters the home, the elder's cultural differences and personal preferences become apparent. The home contains the elder's familiar surroundings, including schedules and routines that may have been maintained for decades.

The physician is a guest in this world; the elder writes the rules and regulations and the physician may feel out of place.

But greater physician interaction adds not only a medical perspective to the team's efforts, but often a continuity that comes from a longstanding relationship with the elder and the family. The physician-patient relationship can be a powerful contribution to the home care team.

Because home care is interdisciplinary, it demands physician skills in teamwork and communication. The physician must know and use the expertise of each professional on the home care team to optimize the quality and efficiency of care.

The increased medical complexity of home care services has created the need for the administrative or advisory physician to evolve into a medical director of home care agencies, a role analogous to the medical director of a nursing home. Quality assurance, protocol development, and clinical staff supervision are among the physician's responsibilities.

The best home care physicians:

1. Are current on available home care, reimbursement policies, and community resources.

2. Identify appropriate patient candidates for home care and make the patient and the family aware of home care options.

3. Certify the elder's need for home care and authorize only the services needed.

4. Anticipate and participate in the elder's hospital discharge planning.

5. Integrate home, office, and hospital to maintain continuity of care, communication, and patient records through the transitions in care settings.

6. Assess the patient's medical, functional, and cognitive status; assess the home for adequacy, safety, and adaptability; assess the caregiver's competency, motivation, and ongoing stress.

7. Provide formal and explicit written orders for home care with specific guidelines about conditions or circumstances that require physician contact.

8. Maintain regular communication with other members of the team.

9. Ensure that the elder and the family caregivers are instructed in and comfortable with their roles in the care plan.

10. Monitor the elder's progress and the home care providers' compliance with the medical care plan.

11. Provide timely response to requests for medical consultation with the team.

12. Maintain the patient's medical records to evaluate quality of care.

Physicians may provide personal assessment and care in the home, especially in management of acutely ill or technology-dependent patients. But the majority of home care is delivered more appropriately and effectively by home care nurses and other therapists under the physician's medical supervision.

Home health agencies must become partners in care. The planning that begins as soon as hospital discharge is considered must continue beyond the elder's return home. Therapy regimens are delivered in the home by physical, speech, and occupational therapists, who also provide the primary physician with ongoing clinical assessments. They perform exercises, teach safe use of equipment, and apply treatments such as ultrasound, health packs, massage, or Transcutaneous Electrical Nerve Stimulation (TENS).

A physical therapist who visits the home can assess the patient and instruct the family on:

1. Reaching realistic goals set by the therapist, patient, and family

2. Using equipment

3. Accomplishing Activities of Daily Living

4. Learning safety procedures

5. Establishing exercise therapy programs

6. Establishing pain relief therapy programs

7. Helping to build a supportive, therapeutic relationship between therapist, family, patient, and community.

Social workers

Social workers are trained professionals who can identify community services, refer the caregiver and the elder to other health care professionals, and offer information about available funding to guide a family through financial crisis. Some are also qualified in psychological counseling.

Home health aides

Home health aides are trained to provide personal care for the elder. Home health aides function much as nurse's aides in the hospital, but they work alone in the elder's home, supervised by a registered nurse.

Home health aides are usually employed by community-based not-for-profit home health agencies or private for-profit agencies. Although home health aides are usually ordered by a doctor as part of the hospital discharge, families can secure health aides on their own through local agencies. Under some circumstances, a primary doctor can prescribe a home health aide, so that fees are paid by Medicare and private insurance. Such payment applies if, for example, the patient needs rehabilitation after a stroke or a broken hip operation, or for restorative care after hospitalization for a debilitating disease.

Visitors programs

Visitors' programs fulfill specific needs for the isolated elder, providing human contact, chore services, and observation of the elder's physical and emotional state.

Those who participate in these programs fill the gap, carrying out functions that are neither precisely health nor social services, require no professional knowledge or skill, and could be performed by a thoughtful neighbor, friend, or relative. On a regular basis the visitor observes or monitors the elder and, in a crisis, is available as an advisor or go-between.

The visitor is a companion and shopper, reader and writer, a sharer of hobbies and gossip. He or she carries out any activity that benefits the patient and strengthens interest in life and human relationships. This companion provides company and services to an elder unable to handle basic Activities of Daily Living. No training is necessary as there is no rendering of medical assistance, just the attention of someone who will do for the isolated elder what he is unable to manage on his own.

Companions may be arranged through a social worker or the Area Agency on Aging in many communities.

Meals on Wheels and nutrition sites

Elders who live alone, and particularly those who are recently bereaved, are at risk of malnutrition. A widow may feel no desire to cook for herself. A widower may be faced with shopping and cooking for the first time in his adult life. Bereavement, loneliness, depression, and apathy about life in general and food in particular can start these elders on a downward cycle.

Meals on Wheels delivers one hot meal daily to an elder who can't leave the house. Nutrition sites provide a hot meal and socialization at a community location, often with transportation provided.

These arrangements, simple as they are, can keep the elder's diet nutritionally sound and enable him to stay in his own home. Good nutrition enhances social and psychological well being.

Companionship at mealtime may be almost as important as the food itself. Many nutritional programs for elders are federally funded through the Older Americans Act of 1965. Others are paid for through community funds, voluntary and civic associations, and professional nonprofits like the Visiting Nurses Association.

Shopping and housekeeping services

Weekly or twice-weekly assistance with grocery shopping and cleaning maintains the elder at home with only minimal assistance.

Escort services

A personal attendant can be hired as needed to escort an elder to medical appointments, shopping, banking, and other errands.

Transportation services

Group or individual transportation can be arranged in most communities for medical appointments, shopping, and social events.

Senior centers

Daily programs, including low-cost lunches, social activities, guest speakers, outings, and other events are offered in even the smallest, most rural communities. Senior centers provide socialization, mental stimulation, and involvement for elders who can leave the house. And they are well connected to agencies providing more extensive services should the need arise.

Continuing education

Programs for elders are offered at local colleges, libraries, and community centers.

Volunteer opportunities

Being able to give of their talents and time to help others boosts elders' self-esteem. Volunteer opportunities are listed in local newspapers and church bulletins, or check hospitals and charitable organizations in your area.

Mental health services

Local agencies can provide counseling for elders with psychiatric disorders, those in crisis, or those with severe emotional distress.

Licensed home health agencies like the Visiting Nurses

Associations are available in most communities to provide skilled services on an intermittent basis. Before signing with any agency, do some research. These 12 questions serve as a good beginning:

1. What services does the company offer?

2. Where is the company located?

3. Does it have a local office?

4. Does it belong to a national network that can service a traveler?

5. Does the company deliver frequent, prompt, reliable service?

6. Is the staff accessible?

7. Is there 24-hour emergency coverage?

8. What are the workers' qualifications?

9. Are they bonded and protected by malpractice insurance?

10. What screening process is used in hiring?

11. Can the company provide references?

12. How does the company expect payment?

Mariah

Widowed and living far from her family, at 76 Mariah had already survived two near-fatal illnesses. Both times, her son and daughter had flown to her bed-side; both times she had beat the odds and returned to independent living. But when she was involved in a minor car accident four years ago, her son, Mark, decided to move in to her home and keep a closer watch over her.

"She insisted she was OK, but she was embarrassed. Embarrassed about being old, I think; embarrassed that people blamed her for the accident. I look back now and wonder if maybe she didn't suffer trauma to the head.

"Anyway, she never drove again after that. And that's when I began to notice odd things around the house. Like silverware put away in the wrong place. Or she'd call me at work and tell me she couldn't find something in the refrigerator. When I got home, whatever she was looking for was right there. Meanwhile, she was skipping lunch out of confusion or frustration or simple forgetfulness.

"She walked to her bank once—a long walk!—and the teller recognized her and drove her home. She'd walk to the beauty shop, the deli, all the places she used to drive to, and then not know how to get home. The morning I woke up and realized she'd already left the house, I knew someone had to be with her 24 hours a day.

"And I decided that someone was me."

"What she has is a form of Alzheimer's, but it's unusual. Until this last hospitalization, she was very ver-

bal, knew her name, address, phone number, birthday. She enjoyed going out with me, visiting friends. She was clear enough to tell me, 'I'm despondent.'

"But without her tranquilizers, she paced. She would move all the furniture in the middle of the night. I had to put a door on the second floor so she couldn't go downstairs without me.

"I bathed her. I changed her when she couldn't control her bowels. I made five small meals for her a day, and I'd feed her if she wouldn't feed herself. But she was wasting away — 'pocketing' her food, particularly meat. That means chewing it but not swallowing, just tucking it in her cheek like a chipmunk and spitting it out later. And she was losing weight."

In the last four months a series of medical problems that began with a fall and ended with respiratory failure has left Mariah immobile, dependent on a respirator and a feeding tube in a hospital for catastrophic care. She weighs 80 pounds, her skin and bones are like paper, and she can no longer speak.

Having seen his mother beat the odds twice before, Mark is not ready to give up. He visits three times a day. He plans how he will care for her when she returns home. Although her quality of life has never been poorer, he believes she still has the will to live, and he will fight for her right to do so.

"I'm a pain to the hospital staff," he admits cheerfully. "I observe, I complain. If I weren't there, she'd have died. I want to be there when they bathe her so they handle her gently. I bribe the nursing staff with muffins or bagels or candy, and I always attach a note: 'Dear staff, Thank you for keeping me comfortable and alive. Mariah.'

"I put cream on her skin, make sure the pillows are just right. I see that the light is dim over her bed and CNN is on the TV day and night. And I do a lot of hand-holding. I'm just trying to stimulate her senses—hearing, seeing, touching — while she's weaned off the respirator.

"These days I'm encouraged when I see her yawn, or hiccup, or try to talk. Those are signs that she's alive." He considers her drawn face on the white pillowcase, her eyes closed, her mouth slack. But he still sees a vibrant spirit in his mother.

"I'm not about to play God for somebody else," Mark says. "My mother has no living will, and she has said she wants to live. I saw my grandmother lose first her dignity and then her life in a nursing home. I swore then that I'd sacrifice my life to keep my mother at home."

ASSESSMENT AND REHABILITATION

8

The first step in a home care plan is a home assessment to identify present or potential risks to the elder's health and overall well-being. A good home care team performs periodic home assessments. Studies show that such intervention significantly reduces hospital admissions and mortality rates.

Do not confuse home assessment with home care. Although evaluation of the home environment may be one element of a home care program, the goal of home care is to treat a particular medical problem. Home assessment, on the other hand, is a diagnostic process aimed at recognizing aspects of the elder's home life that compromise quality of life. Its purpose is to organize services to deal with a defined medical problem, integrating the pieces into an individualized, comprehensive management plan that optimizes the elder's quality of life and chances of remaining at home.

As caregiver to someone who probably enjoyed a busy, independent earlier life, how can you know what help is needed? Where do you get the necessary support? How do you know when an elder still living independently might benefit from a home assessment?

There are seven clues:

1. Advancing age

2. Psychiatric symptoms

3. Nonspecific physical symptoms

4. Dementia

5. Vision defects

6. Increasing number of illnesses

7. Functional impairment

Whatever his disability, the elder needs to be involved in life. Remaining active both mentally and physically keeps the elder in the best health, and can even abate or reverse disabilities that seemed permanent.

Home care emphasizes what the elder can do. The rest comes about after abilities have been assessed.

Home visits help the caregiver adjust community-based services to the elder's changing needs and ensure that he continues to receive them. Recommendations might include initiating or increasing home help, adding home equipment aids, or modifying the home.

Services may be added or removed as the elder's status changes, but the rule never changes: The patient must always be encouraged to do all he can independently. When family caregivers understand the anguish of an elder who realizes he will never again function at full capacity, they tend to be more creative and sensitive about maintaining the elder's independence. This is where a home health care team is invaluable. It is teamwork that will keep the elder out of an institution and comfortably at home.

Problems identified through a home visit are grouped according to safety, psychobehavior, family stress, nutrition, Activities of Daily Living, finances, and medical problems. They can be defined in four categories:

1. **Health assessment:** Identification of illness and functional capabilities, including appraisal of health behaviors, physical impairment, nutritional status, illnesses, medications, and possible alternative therapies.

2. **Environmental assessment:** Consideration of safety and comfort features that allow the elder to function optimally. Will stairs be a problem? Is there access to a bathroom, and can it be used safely and independently? If the elder is in a wheelchair, is the home accessible, inside and out, including ramped elevations and door widths of at least 30 inches?

3. **Social assessment:** Identification of the elder's family responsibilities; his support network, including the family caregiver's abilities and disabilities and the presence of nuclear or extended family; the elder's knowledge and use of community resources, neighbors, and church; and his financial resources.

4. **Interaction assessment:** Evaluation of how the elder can and will interact with each of the factors listed above as necessary to diminish or enhance his quality of life.

A comprehensive geriatric assessment helps the physician choose the right medication and dosage, taking into consideration the nutritional assessment. Underweight elders, for example, have a greater risk of drug side effects. Medications can impact on nutritional status by affecting appetite, food absorption, and metabolism.

Home from the hospital

Home health care is a valuable and viable option for families who don't want to rely on a nursing home for recuperative care, which often becomes permanent care.

Returning home from the hospital is nevertheless an emotional experience. The warmth and convenience of home are certainly more inviting than the hospital and its routines, but patients returning home in fragile health are a relatively new phenomenon.

Sometimes when physicians feel their patients are ready to be released from the hospital, caregiver families feel unprepared and uncertain about their ability to deal with their elder's problems alone.

At the same time, even after years of independent living, elders who have been hospitalized often consider the hospital a safe and secure cocoon. Their needs are met, the trained staff understands their illness, and they feel unconditional acceptance in the hospital. The longer they remain, the harder for them to believe they can manage at home without professional support. In-home rehabilitation guards against professional dependence and increases patient confidence.

Rehabilitation is a restorative process that helps an ill or handicapped person regain maximum physical, mental, economic, and vocational usefulness. It often follows hospitalization.

Because rehabilitation requires the coordinated efforts of many health care professionals, a team approach is mandatory. Of course the elder and his family are central to the team. Even with lifelong disability, the goal is maximum personal independence with minimum dependence on health care professionals.

Discharge planning should begin the day of hospital admission. The discharge planner in many hospitals is a medical social worker, discharge coordinator, or public health nurse who is trained to determine the aftercare needs of the patient and the resources available in the community. In many instances the discharge planner is also the home care planner.

When discharge becomes part of the elder's medical plan, the patient, family, and others participating in the home care program should also become part of the elder's medical plan, watching recommended videotapes and attending meetings and training sessions available through the hospital. The patient's entire support system will need time to adjust to the new agenda to provide a smooth transition to home care.

Some recommended topics for a going-home program include:

- Activities of Daily Living

- Skin care, bathing, and oral care

- Positioning and moving in bed

- Pain control

- Bowel and bladder control

- Ostomy care

- Massage

- Exercise

- Nutrition

- Recreation

Emergencies at home

A visit to the patient's home before discharge can help the discharge planner anticipate problems and needs before the patient's arrival. Studies show that for a significant number of elders, a home visit by a geriatric nurse or other specialist identifies important problems not noted at the physician's initial office evaluation. On the other hand, a visit shortly after discharge may help reassess needs after the patient and family have had the opportunity to adapt to the new home routines.

The rehabilitation team teaches the elder to use all his abilities to the fullest so that, within his limits, he can be a useful member of society. The elder learns to control his life, direct others in his care, and seek appropriate medical and professional services when needed.

In the home, the elder is in familiar surroundings and family members can actively participate in his recuperation. In addition, home rehabilitation is less costly than an inpatient program.

Because the goal of rehabilitation is to help patients be as independent and safe as possible at home, the home is the natural setting for rehabilitation. Many elders become confused and insecure in new surroundings and cannot perform to their potential. At home, they are happier, more motivated, and able to reach higher functional levels more quickly. An occupational therapist assessing Activities of Daily Living, accessibility of the home, and hand and arm manipulation of objects can eliminate confusion and attain higher function with home rehabilitation.

Relearning movement patterns and learning to use adaptive equipment when performing customary tasks also happens more quickly and is more meaningful in familiar surroundings. An example: Homemakers asked to work in the kitchens they have used for 20 years display positive self-images and are more motivated to become independent.

In the home, the occupational therapist can find solutions for real-life situations. Teaching new ways to transport laundry, the therapist incorporates energy conservation, joint protection, and work simplification into the task. The therapist may work with an architect, designer, or carpenter to eliminate physical barriers.

Ramps, grab bars, widened doorways, and specially designed furniture can make the difference between a functionally safe or unsafe independent life.

Testing the patient's strength, posture, flexibility, and balance identifies underlying problems that may contribute to a loss of function. Again, this testing best occurs within the context of functional activities and the patient's usual routine. For example, lower extremity strength and balance can be assessed during ambulation, transfers, or stooping to reach for objects in the kitchen. Note that the emphasis is on functional performance and energy conservation.

Another advantage to working within the home is the ability to distinguish between true deficit and situational deficit.

Home rehabilitation enlists the family into active participation, treats physical and psychosocial issues, and creates a care plan unique to the elder's home.

In-home assessments identify areas of potential support early, thereby avoiding or alleviating typical rehab problems that stem from patient fragility and family helplessness. Some of the questions that can be answered during an in-home assessment:

1. How is the family organized? Who is expected to do what?

2. What is the crisis or major stressor they face?

3. What is the family's experience in coping with change or crisis?

4. What is the timing of the current change or crisis?

5. What resources are available to the family?

6. What is the relationship between family structure and function?

The family must support and encourage independence, not rush to take over. There is no point in rehabilitation staff spending months to retrain an elder if well-meaning relatives do everything for him at home. Why does this occur so regularly?

Perhaps the family isn't aware of the patient's ability. Perhaps the elder, who might walk perfectly for the physiotherapist, is frightened and confused away from the hospital setting. Family members should talk to the rehabilitation staff and learn how to help the elder, creating a bridge between hospital and home.

They need to have a clear idea of the elder's endurance and strength from the doctor or home health care team, and be guided by that evaluation. Strength and endurance are often the major limiting factors in an elder's ability to maintain independence.

Goal setting is important, but the steps need to be small and readily achievable to give the elder a sense of accomplishment.

As he experiences success, his goals can increase. Self-care goals—brushing his teeth, combing his hair, feeding himself, making himself comfortable in bed—are all excellent morale builders. Small, steady increases in exercise are also good for mind and body alike.

The family must also bear in mind that the elder's struggle to maintain independence is exhausting for him and his caregivers. Losing ground is inevitable, as is the depression that follows. The home care team needs to accept that and move on, setting new goals and achieving other levels of success.

The rehabilitation nurse is the quarterback in home rehabilitation, coordinating and overseeing the team on a daily basis. The nurse makes sure the plans created at team meetings are implemented. And the nurse is the teacher, instructing the elder on living safely and comfortably in his home in light of his disease and his treatments. Too often, for example, the elder does not understand his medication's effects and side effects. A good nurse/teacher explains his prescriptions and sees that he follows his drug program.

Technological advances have shifted even sophisticated and complex care back to the home. Simple, safe, reliable, and portable instruments and clinical equipment have greatly enhanced diagnostic, therapeutic, and monitoring functions in home care.

Conditions like diabetes, hypertension, and obstructive pulmonary disease require frequent monitoring. User-friendly devices make it possible for elders or their caregivers to monitor treatments and disease activity themselves, but the use of these home monitors requires education and training if the information and results are to be accurate.

In practice, the family can duplicate much of the equipment of an institutional hospital in the home. Caregivers can get a complete electric hospital bed, trapeze, oxygen tank, suction equipment, bedside commode, wheelchair, and other rental equipment from hospital supply sources. They can obtain surgical dressings, sterile gloves, necessary tools, gastrostomy tubes, and other special hospital supplies.

All that is unique about institutional care is the myth that the aged can best be cared for there. That is true in fewer instances than you may realize.

Stewart ──────────────────────

Stewart Logan is a gentleman, but he can't help glancing down at his watch; it's 3:30, and he always takes his third one-mile walk of the day at 3. But he's got a visitor sitting at the tiny round table by the window in the Bide-Awhile Retirement Home, so he continues their chat.

"I was in the hospital for congestive heart failure every four or five months back in '91," he recalls. "Once I had a heart attack, then a stroke and then another heart attack before they released me. But the doctors didn't tell me about restricted diets. I'd get out of the hospital and go right back to eating the same stuff, like it never happened. If I wanted pizza, I had a pizza—do you know how much salt is in a pizza?"

Today, Stewart is well aware of dietary restrictions, the dangers of smoking, the need to watch medication, and the benefits of exercise. He is impatient with the residents around him who can't or won't take care of themselves.

"My roommate is killing himself," Stewart says by way of example. "He walks from the bathroom or the dining room, and he can't get his breath. And as soon as he can breathe again, out he goes for a smoke.

"I'm glad I quit," he says. "When cigarettes got up to 25 cents a pack, that was it for me!"

Stewart lives at the Bide-Awhile because it's not far from his daughter's home, and he is an important part of their family. He's a loyal fan of his son-in-law's over-50 softball team, and never misses a day at the track when the family's horse runs.

He's included in cookouts and holiday parties and goes along when they make the five-hour drive to see their grandchildren. Stewart says a trip like that would kill most of the people in the Bide-Awhile.

Truth to tell, watching a seven-inning softball game can take a lot out of Stewart. That's why he exercises. "My long walks keep me balanced to where, if they say go, I'm ready," he explains. "I know I'm living on borrowed time, so any time I get a chance to do something, I'm going to do it. No sense sitting here feeling sorry for myself."

His doctor would tell you that Stewart Logan seems to have stopped the aging process. His daughter say he wasn't expected to live six months when she first settled him into the retirement home. She was warned he'd require 24-hour supervision because his mind was gone. Today he's devised his own system to keep track of the 17 prescriptions he takes, the vials lined up and marked in his top dresser drawer. The tally sheets of a running game of gin rummy with his roommate are stacked neatly by the window. And he hasn't been in a hospital in four years.

"There's nothing wrong with his mind," Stewart's daughter laughs. "He's wonderful. A little cranky sometimes, and spoiled rotten, but no trouble. But I'm fortunate; not everyone has it as easy."

"Not many have a good family to turn to," responds her father.

THE ACTIVE ELDER

Activity is important to each of us, regardless of age. But a sedentary lifestyle aggravates the loss of physical capacity that accompanies aging. Activity is the only way to prevent wasting away, the only way to maintain the physical capacity for strength, speed, and coordination that is so important to the elder.

Motion increases blood circulation, which improves function of all body parts, particularly the cardiovascular and respiratory systems. Motion also helps maintain and even increase the range of motion in joints, prevents deformities by keeping joints moving, maintains and increases muscle strength following sickness and injury, aids healing, and prevents swollen feet and legs and skin breakdown.

Other benefits of regular exercise include:

- Improved oxygen consumption during exertion, for better conditioning
- Lowered heart rate while resting, so organs work more efficiently
- Increased muscle tone
- Decreased body fat

- Maintaining flexible joints

- Reduced blood pressure

- Release of muscular tension

- Reduced pain

- Increased strength and mobility

Regular exercise makes smooth, relaxed movement habitual and prevents "contractures," or permanent shortening of muscles, tendons and scar tissue. Contractures cause elders to move and do less and feel uncomfortable. Aging slows all body activities. Unless a plan of activity is carried out, an elder loses more and more of his ability to perform all motion.

Exercise need not be painful and should not loom as a hated chore to be endured. Attitude affects physical therapy: The greater the elder's initiative, self-motivation, and positive attitude, the more effective the therapy.

The goal should be to replace range-of-motion repetitions with walking, performing household activities, or swimming, thereby increasing not only function but socialization, self-image, and body awareness. Physical therapy should involve the safe, consistent, and effective completion of purposeful tasks. Mastery of exacting movements and completion of artificial tasks is not necessary.

To help the elder become as independent as possible, an exercise program may include any combination of the following:

- Range-of-motion exercises

- Activities of Daily Living

- A Hubbard tank, whirlpool bath, ultrasound, hot wax bath or other special procedures

- Occupational therapy

- Recreational therapy

The bedridden

Being in bed for a few days, for even the most minor illness, causes old but otherwise healthy joints to stiffen and muscles to weaken. When the patient decides to get out of bed, he will depend on others for assistance in walking and transferring. Recuperation progresses slowly, as disability and pain make mobility very difficult.

But instead of recognizing that this atrophy is the natural result of short- or long-term disuse, the elder and the family may decide the patient is not ready to get out of bed. They may even decide the patient's health is getting worse, since the joint and muscle pain wasn't a problem before the bed rest. So it's back to bed, where the stiffness eventually turns into inertia and permanent deformity.

The danger of inactivity

Without physical activity, protein breaks down and calcium leaks from the bones. Eventually the bones soften and fracture easily. Muscles shrink in size and strength, atrophying. There is decreased flexibility and strength, and a loss of speed and coordination. Endurance is markedly decreased. The bedridden patient is prone to pneumonia, blood clots, and bedsores.

If severe illness and disability inhibit all movement, great care must be taken to turn and position the bedridden elder for maximum comfort and to prevent skin breakdown. A constant watch should be kept. An elder must change bed position at least every two hours; if he can't do so unassisted, the caregiver must make movement a priority and turn the patient every time care is provided. This attention must continue around the clock if the patient does not naturally shift his position while sleeping.

Bedsores, also called "pressure sores" or "decubitus ulcers," can appear within days of immobilization. They occur when the weight of the body reduces the blood supply to one area of the body, usually where the bone is near the surface. The elder's skin is often fragile and thin, and some elders are inadequately cushioned with fat. The buttocks are especially susceptible, as are the elbows, heels, toes, and hips.

What should a caregiver look for? First the skin reddens slightly and becomes inflamed, and tissue cells die. Then small skin breaks appear. Untreated, the break deteriorates deeper into layers of skin and then to muscle, tendon, and bone. Each layer becomes infected and damaged, and the bone may become visible.

Neglected bedsores are not only painful, but can become so infected they require hospitalization. Bedsores have even been known to cause death.

Once a sore progresses beyond the early stages of skin breakdown, it can take months for new tissue to grow back, even with the best treatment. Bedsores can be a tremendous problem in home nursing, due to the imperfect facilities in most homes, lack of outside help and, sometimes, a heavy invalid. The best treatment for bedsores is a commitment to prevent them.

Skin care is mandatory. Each time the elder is turned, rub the areas in danger. Supervise proper hygiene; encourage daily bathing to stimulate skin and prevent skin breakdown. Pressure can be relieved with special padding. Caregivers should watch for areas of red, shiny skin that lack sensation. These are the first signs of skin breakdown.

Those most susceptible to bedsores are:

- Long-term bedridden or wheelchair-bound patients

- Patients with poor circulation

- Diabetics

- Incontinent patients

- Patients wearing appliances, bandages, or traction devices

- Patients who cannot manage proper hygiene

- Patients with sensation losses

If your elder is bedridden and not wholly paralyzed, he needs to be taught how to range his joints with the goal of eventually sitting, then standing. Prolonged rest causes contractures, exemplified by the toe-walking position common in bedridden people.

It may seem easiest to leave the elder alone rather than insist on movement, especially if he objects strenuously. But leaving him alone invites increased disability, bedsores, infection, and markedly diminished mental alertness. The bedridden patient's condition does not remain static. Without expert nursing, the condition deteriorates and more problems arise.

Even the most loving family will find it difficult to stop a bedridden patient from deteriorating. And the longer he is allowed to lie in bed or sit in a chair, the longer before he regains normal muscle strength and a more active life.

For the bedridden elder, simple movement, preferably by the elder himself, is the most important factor. Physical mobility includes the ability to move in bed and to "transfer," and eventually to move about.

Transfer

The ability to transfer—from bed to wheelchair, wheelchair to toilet, wheelchair to tub or shower, sitting to standing, and wheelchair to automobile—is key to independence. Even a non-ambulatory patient in a wheelchair who can transfer on his own can be independent. For many elders, the transition from sitting to standing is the most difficult.

Using the correct equipment helps: A freestanding bed that is hip level to the caregiver can make a huge difference in administering to a bedridden patient. A trapeze positioned above the patient allows the patient to make himself comfortable and transfer in and out of the bed, or it simply aids the person lifting and moving him.

A physical or occupational therapist can show the caregiver proper body mechanics to avoid injury to caregiver or elder during a transfer to and from a wheelchair. Briefly, the caregiver will be instructed to:

1. Lock the wheelchair wheels. The chair must not move during transfer.

2. Maintain a straight back, with hips and knees bent.

3. Be sure the elder can see the surface to which he is transferring.

Moving to mobility

Mobility begins with "range of motion"—the ordinary movements of the large muscle groups and joints—and advances to strength, endurance, coordination, balance, and freedom from pain. It encompasses the ability to direct one's movement, hold one's body in a designated position, and prevent unwanted movement.

For the caregiver, the important issue is helping the patient not only to participate but to develop a sense of responsibility, independence, and initiative toward increasing vigor. It is all part of encouraging an active attitude toward life. The amount of energy the elder can mobilize will help determine the outcome of his physical therapy.

Physical exercise benefits even the very elderly. Studies find that even frail patients in their late 80s or 90s get around more quickly, climb stairs better, and have even been known to abandon their walkers after a few weeks of lifting weights to strengthen their legs.

The benefits of exercise

It is never too late to reap the benefits of fitness. Most of us are unduly negative about what those at the end of their lives can physically accomplish. We must all be more optimistic. Working aging muscles strengthens them, and extra strength improves quality of life. Those who are physically active every day are less depressed, more mobile, and more likely to participate in activities.

Regular exercise increases maximum oxygen consumption, improving conditioning. Exercise lowers the heart rate and improves circulation, so other organs work less. Exercise decreases blood pressure, burns excess body fat, and improves strength and mobility. Exercise keeps joints and muscles supple. Exercise makes anyone feel better, and empowers self-worth and well-being.

Exercise needs to be approached sensibly. Elders need alternate periods of rest and activity. They need to keep joints as comfortable as possible. In general, elders should not stand for long periods, lift heavy weights, climb stairs unnecessarily, or do strenuous overhead stretching. Elders with arthritis should control their weight to avoid excessive strain on joints.

Is *he safe?*

Take a good look at a chair-bound elder's environment before urging him to be more active. If he is mobile, is he safe? Falls are the most common accident in home care. How is the living space arranged? If he were able to move around more easily, would he enjoy more independence? What basic changes—railings, rearranged furniture, bathroom safety devices—would increase his independence? Can he move in bed, rise from various chairs, propel a wheelchair or walker? Is there access to bathrooms? Can he navigate doorways, thresholds, rugs? Are stairs becoming more difficult? Is he safe around crowds or pets? Can he get into the car?

Once his space is open and safe, encourage the elder in basic range-of-motion exercises. Too often a temporarily incapacitated elder never attempts to resume normal daily activities—sitting, standing, walking, bending, and reaching—that naturally put the body's joints through their full range of motion dozens of times a day.

The ankles, knees, and hips are most likely to stiffen in the bedridden, but range-of-motion exercises should involve the shoulders, elbows, wrists, fingers, and thumbs as well. All joints should be ranged for up to ten repetitions once or twice a day. Begin with three repetitions, increasing them as tolerance permits. Take each movement as far as the joint will go, with a little extra effort to take it one step further.

Initially, range-of-motion exercises are done in bed to produce little strain on the elder. They consist of arm, elbow, and leg lifts; bends and stretches; and wrist and ankle rotations. If the elder is too weak to accomplish these exercises alone, a caregiver can be taught how to assist by the home health nurse or physical therapist.

Ranging can be undertaken while the patient is lying or sitting. An excellent time is during the daily bath. The caregiver should help only with ranges he cannot do on his own.

When the caregiver helps

Choose the joint to be ranged. Support the extremity above and below the joint with your hands. For example, support the arm beneath the elbow while ranging the shoulder. Gently, slowly, and steadily move the part of the body farthest from the patient through a complete range of motions. When ranging the knee, lift and support the thigh with one hand. With the other hand on the calf (the part farthest from the patient), slowly bend and straighten the leg five to ten times.

Ranging every joint this way should take no more than ten minutes. Make certain not to cause pain or force motion. Avoid sudden moves, and heed patient complaints of pain or fatigue.

When the patient is strong enough, he should try these exercises alone. Initially, the joints and extremities should be supported by the bed to eliminate the extra burden of gravity. The next goal is to range the joints without the support of the bed. Eventually, resistance should be added to the exercise, with weights added to the patient's arms and legs or with manual resistance by the caregiver.

The caregiver should take a tip from professional therapists: If you are convinced the exercises will greatly improve the patient's health and well being, your positive expectations can be a self-fulfilling prophecy: They raise the patient's expectations and make him work harder, which makes him improve in body, mind, and spirit. Again, the goal is independence in small steps.

When the elder can spend part of his day sitting in a chair, home exercise should advance to head rolls, shoulder shrugs, large and small arm circles, back stretches and bends, pelvic tilts, knee-to-chest stretches, and curl downs. The elder who can do 10 to 20 repetitions is ready to spend the day out of bed and walking around, resuming many of his normal daily activities.

Once he is sitting up, don't allow your elder to relapse to a prone position; once standing, don't allow him to rely entirely on the chair or wheelchair. Make your elder aware of the dangers of immobility.

Assistive devices

Sometimes decreased sensation, balance, vision, flexibility, or strength makes locomotion difficult. Or accident or illness can result in temporary or permanent loss of function. Such an elder should be evaluated for assistive devices and/or equipment that compensates for lost function and enhances the independence of those with impairments, disabilities, or handicaps.

The World Health Organization defines "impairment" as an actual injury, disease, or other disorder that produces a reduction in physical or mental function. The impairment becomes a "disability" when the restriction impedes the person's functional capacity. It becomes a "handicap" when the person's social role is affected. Assistive devices and equipment may help keep an impairment from becoming a disability or a handicap.

Mobility aids—canes, walkers, crutches, leg braces, and wheelchairs—increase stability, facilitate movement, decrease pain, protect joints, and conserve energy. They may be prescribed for various reasons:

1. To replace lost body parts or special senses.

2. To replace function totally and permanently lost from either weakness or loss of range of motion.

3. To encourage early motion and function following injury or disease in order to prevent atrophy, maintain muscle strength, and prevent loss of range of motion.

4. To provide positioning and support of weakened areas of the body. By maintaining body alignment, such devices prevent permanent loss of power in overstretched and overfatigued muscles and possible permanent deformity.

5. To increase function of residual muscle power and skill involved in various motions.

6. To assist in control of incoordination or spasms.

7. To minimize the assistance needed from others when complete independence is not possible.

The elder's doctor may recommend adaptive equipment and training in Activities of Daily Living to help him learn new ways to feed, dress, groom, and assist himself in the bathroom. A physical therapist can also evaluate and suggest ambulation techniques. It is important that the elder use the right appliance, that it be adjusted to the right size and configuration, and that both the elder and the family review its use and suitability.

A cane should come to hip bone level and be rubber tipped. A three-pointed cane offers additional stability. A walker offers even more support and can be fitted with wheels—if the patient knows how to use it. Walkers must be planted firmly one step ahead, then stepped into. When the elder is standing and stable, he repeats the process. Too many elders take a step while holding the walker off the ground, accounting for many falls.

Until he is steady on his feet, an elder learning to rely on a cane or walker needs a "spotter." This person stands close behind with a firm hand on the small of the elder's back or holding his belt. If the elder starts to fall, the sudden jolt of someone catching him may injure them both. A good spotter breaks the fall by slowly guiding the elder safely to the floor, bending the knees, not the back.

Advanced exercise: walking

A regular exercise program that builds stamina and muscle tone usually begins with walking. It requires no special equipment and can be undertaken almost anywhere. Walking, biking, and swimming are excellent ways to build strength and endurance. Any exercise should begin with passive and gentle limbering and stretching.

No exercise program should be undertaken without physician approval. These basics are usually recommended for the elder exerciser:

1. Exercise every day. Sporadic exercising offers no benefit.

2. Adhere to a specific time as much as possible.

3. Perform exercises on a firm, comfortable surface in the same place every day.

4. Wear comfortable, loose clothing.

5. Begin with a brief relaxation exercise and perform all exercises slowly and smoothly.

6. Expect the mild stiffness and soreness that appears after the first exercise to dissipate within three or four days.

7. Record your progress!

A daily activity record is perhaps the most important part of the regimen. It gives the elder concrete evidence of progress and confidence in his ability to again use his body.

Walking tips To get the most out of walking, the elder should:

1. Walk with head high, not watching his feet.

2. Consciously relax the muscles of his arms, shoulders, and neck.

3. Come down on the heel of the foot and rock forward to drive off the ball of the foot.

4. Choose a comfortable length of stride.

5. Begin with short walks and build endurance by gradually increasing time and distance.

6. Move at a comfortable pace, with no attention to speed.

7. Check muscle tension as he walks, relaxing again when he feels any increased tightness, particularly in the neck and shoulders.

8. Slow down if pain or discomfort develops. If the symptoms continue, he should stop the walking regimen and see his doctor.

I would be remiss if I did not mention T'ai Chi Ch'uan in any discussion of exercise. Some call it the "old people's exercise," because its graceful, meditative stretching movements limber the body, tone the muscles, and release tension.

Considered a healing exercise, the Oriental method employs a series of postures or stances and hand movements linked together like a string of words in a sentence. There are between 27 and 156 T'ai Chi Ch'uan movements, depending on the form studied.

More information on T'ai Chi is available in bookstores and libraries, and many local community classes teach it. T'ai Chi Ch'uan can become a way of life.

Relaxation exercises

You may think relaxation is passive, an absence of action, but the tension of tight back muscles or mental stress can be reduced only by taking action. Relaxation exercises are a major weapon for relieving pain, promoting well-being, and prolonging life.

As physical conditioning relieves pain-creating tension in the body, mental relaxation exercises erase tension and stress. Mental relaxation exercises—creative visualization, guided imagery, meditation—enable the elder to momentarily escape his surroundings and concentrate on relieving body tension. The following exercises require only a floor exercise mat and a small pillow or rolled towel:

1. **For upper body tension:** Stand erect with feet apart and hands behind your neck, elbows extended to each side. Bend the upper portion of the body to the side, first to the

right and hold for five seconds, then to the left for five seconds. Repeat several times.

2. **For head, neck, and shoulder muscles**: Lie on back, hands tucked under the small of the back, palms down. Lift head, shoulders, and elbows off the floor while tightening abdominal muscles. Hold for five seconds and return to the mat. Repeat several times.

3. **For relaxation**: Sit comfortably in a quiet room, eyes closed, and inhale deeply. Hold your breath for three seconds. Now exhale slowly, saying a simple or meaningless sound like "ohm" or "love." At the end of the exhalation, stomach should be moderately contracted and body slightly sagging, as though it were sinking. Repeat five times.

Keith

Keith and Joan worked hard for 40 years, raised a family, got ahead, saved for the retirement that would be their just reward.

At age 65 they exchanged careers for golf, travel, entertaining old friends, and planning their future.

But an earlier brush with cancer reared its ugly head again, and this time Joan didn't respond as quickly or as well. She fought for two years before dying, leaving Keith wiped out emotionally and financially. At 71 he felt out of control, betrayed, bitter.

Their ritual cocktail hour was his salvation as well as a cruel reminder of how much he missed his wife and the life they had planned for. Their busy social life had dwindled, and friends came around less frequently. Keith's drinking increased.

When his doctor saw how anxious and shaky Keith was, she prescribed a low dose of Valium. Keith was soon washing a double dose down with gin. When the doctor questioned his need for a prescription refill, Keith said he'd dropped the bottle and lost most of them.

Then he made an appointment with another doctor, telling himself he just wanted to make sure he had enough Valium on hand to get over the tough times.

The signs were there, if someone were looking for them. Levels of alcohol in bottles dropped alarmingly. There were empties in the morning's trash. Keith's speech was slurred during evening phone calls. He passed out in front of the TV most evenings. But Keith was a decent man going through difficult time. If he was drinking a little, who could blame him? If his patterns of living were drastically different, there was good reason for it.

"Alcoholism in the elderly slips by," says Randee Iman, a psychiatric and addiction nurse who now works in the home care field. "People don't think of the elderly as alcoholics. Even medical people don't pick up on it. Doctors even recommend a drink for elder patients who seem anxious. And in many families, alcoholism is not something anyone wants to talk about. Every family has had alcohol trouble of some kind, and there is fear, and resentment, and shame. Lots of shame."

The best hope for Keith is family or friends who are able to get him to see that his drinking, once seemingly the solution, has become the problem. Sometimes getting visitors or hired help in the house on a regular basis turns things around. Sometimes getting the patient active, whether in golf, or volunteer work, or a community meal site, or day care, gets him back on track, too busy to knock himself out with prescriptions and alcohol.

"And sometimes the answer is a nursing home," Iman says. "They hate that, but sometimes they aren't safe to be home alone. That's why it's so important for family and friends to be aware of the dangers of alcohol for the elderly, and to get help if they are worried.

"I've been called in when a patient was having a couple of beers every night, and after assessing her I've been able to say, 'She's OK. Don't worry.' But I'd sure rather do that than have to hospitalize some poor guy because no one bothered to get involved until it was too late.

"Alcoholism can happen to anyone," warns Iman, "and it's a sad and unnecessary way to end a long and otherwise respectable life."

MANAGING PAIN 10

Pain is a different phenomenon at home than it is within an institution. At home, pain relief relies heavily on symptom management. In-home chronic pain techniques can be especially effective because they allow the elder to take responsibility for his own pain management.

However, in-home pain management presents caregivers with special problems. Pain management may require potent drugs that must be monitored carefully to achieve maximum pain control with minimum side effects. High-tech pain strategies such as morphine pumps and chronic spinal infusions also require special knowledge and skills.

Pain is universal yet individual. For management purposes, it helps to distinguish acute pain from chronic pain. Acute pain is related to an underlying condition and responds to short-term analgesic medications and treatment of the condition. Chronic pain, on the other hand, has no clear-cut origin. It is of long duration, has many contributing factors, and requires a multidisciplinary approach in both assessment and management.

An elder with chronic pain should be evaluated for functional impairment and psychological problems. His ability to move around and do things for himself may be compromised. The anxiety and depression that accompany long-term, unrelieved chronic pain cannot be overemphasized.

Pain management in the home

Reliance on family caregivers, limited access to diagnostic facilities, and poor pharmacy services can all influence home pain management.

We assume that a comfortable home environment is more conducive to pain management. The fact is, in-home treatment may not result in the most effective pain management. Studies estimate that 25 to 50 percent of elders who live in their communities suffer significant pain problems. Results include depression, decreased socialization, sleep disturbance, impaired ambulation, and increased use and cost of health care services. Other geriatric conditions aggravated by pain include gait disturbances, falls, slow rehabilitation, polypharmacy, cognitive dysfunction, and malnutrition.

For the caregiver, the burden of pain management includes:

1. Demands on time

2. Emotional adjustment

3. Distressing symptoms

4. Work adjustment

5. Sleep adjustment

6. Family/relationship adjustment

The home care team needs to be aware of the caregiver burden associated with pain management and help establish a plan of care that considers the skills and resources available. That may mean simplified medication regimens and longer-acting analgesics.

Something as simple as a leisurely visit with friends or

grandchildren can greatly decrease pain, as can prayer, meditation, and music. Physical methods include heat, cold, and massage. Physical therapy that stretches and strengthens specific muscles and joints will decrease muscle spasm and improve functional activity, and usually reduce pain.

Transcutaneous Electrical Nerve Stimulation (TENS) has been used in a variety of chronic pain conditions in elders. Because placement of the electrodes and adjustment of the current must be precise, an experienced therapist should initiate and train home care elders and their caregivers on proper TENS therapy.

Psychological maneuvers, including biofeedback, relaxation, and hypnosis, can help elders who have high levels of cognitive function. And of course activities, exercise, and recreation should be encouraged. Inactivity and immobility may contribute extensively to depression and pain.

Alternatives in pain reduction

Heat is often recommended to lessen pain and muscle stiffness and to prepare certain patients for physical therapy. Heat therapy should be applied for no more than 20 minutes at a time. Heat therapies that work best in the home:

- **Hydrocollator packs**—sophisticated heating pads made from canvas and filled with silica gel and contoured to fit the body.

- **Infrared heat lamps**—radiate heat onto specific areas

- **Paraffin baths**—containers of warm melted wax into which the patient dips his hands or feet for arthritis pain relief.

- **Ultrasound**—high-frequency waves that penetrate tissue with a unique deep heat.

- **Whirlpools**—swirl warm water currents around an immersed body part, massaging joints or easing discomfort from a fracture.

- **A hot bath**—one of the oldest, easiest, and most comforting heat therapies.

Physicians may prescribe cold therapy to reduce swelling, spasticity, or inflammation. Cold therapy is usually the application of ice.

Medication management in the home

Pharmacotherapy is perhaps the most important component in medical management for the elder. Like pain management, it differs in the home than in other health care settings. The main responsibility for properly administering drugs rests on the elder or the caregiver, with limited supervision by health care professionals.

Life is less regimented in the home. Meals are not necessarily served at predetermined times, making it more difficult to avoid interactions between drugs and food.

Furthermore, home care elders may have severe functional limitations that produce difficulties in the procurement or handling of medications. Multiple prescriptions, the inability to read prescription labels, difficulty in opening medication containers or dissecting tablets, inaccessibility to the drug store, and financial problems can all affect the success of medication therapy. Drug store deliveries, mail-order prescriptions, and compliance aids that remind the elder to take drugs all help.

A Visiting Nurse Association study showed that almost half the home care patients surveyed were taking five or more different prescription medications. Data suggests that the health of elders in home care settings would be improved through better medication management strategies.

A medication assessment is the first step. It starts with a complete drug history from both the patient's and physician's perspective. A list of drugs available to the patient is made and the appropriateness of the medication is assessed with these questions:

1. Are all drugs currently necessary? Has the primary indication been resolved?

2. Is there a diagnosis for each drug?

3. Is each drug effective?

4. Are some drugs prescribed to treat the side effects of other drugs?

5. Are dosages adjusted to the patient's age and weight?

6. Are dosages adjusted to the patient's ability to absorb or process the drug?

7. Are there side effects that might be particularly troublesome to this patient?

8. Have drug-drug and drug-disease interactions been identified, and the drug therapy adjusted accordingly?

9. Are drugs monitored by serum drug concentrations?

10. Can administration be reduced to once or twice a day through longer-acting drugs?

The family caregiver plays an important role in pain management. Her health, attitude, and knowledge have a profound effect on the successful management of the elder's chronic medical problems.

Some factors in her control include:

1. Deciding how to comfort the elder and what medications to administer

2. Determining when to administer medications

3. Serving night duty to administer medications

4. Reminding the patient to take drugs and encouraging medication compliance

5. Controlling activities and treatment

6. Guarding against the potential misuse of medications

Substance abuse in the elderly

With all of our preconceived notions about elders, we rarely see them as alcoholics. Yet 2.5 million of our elders are drinking themselves to death. They are alcoholics, their final years wasted and their lives cut short. Experts estimate that 15 to 20 percent of our elders abuse alcohol, many of them drinking later in life due to a crisis or age-related stresses.

One important reason is loss of social contact and a sense of isolation. A 1992 report by a Congressional Subcommittee on Health estimated that in 1990 alcohol-related hospital costs for elders approached $60 million. Up to 70 percent of hospitalized elders have some alcohol-related illnesses.

The signs of alcoholism mirror those of aging: unexplained falls and bruises, memory loss, trembling, weight loss, fatigue, insomnia, a desire for isolation.

Alcoholism is the most common substance abuse among the elderly, but not the only one. Memory loss and disorientation often blamed on Alzheimer's could in fact be attributed to excessive drugs.

Medications prescribed or taken *ad lib* by elders from over-the-counter sources can confuse them and contribute to alcohol abuse.

And many elders abuse prescription drugs, a pattern that begins with emotional difficulties or confusion and memory loss. Frequently, the elder's family is unaware of their parent's problem.

Addressing substance abuse within the family is never easy. The first step is to understand and clarify the situation. Then the family can explore the issues involved. Here are a few ways the family can offer a helping hand to an elder suspected of abusing alcohol or prescribed drugs:

1. Call at different times, both day and evening. When does the elder slur his speech?

2. Avoid communication when he is drinking. If he drinks in the evening, talk earlier in the day.

3. Be loving and gentle, not confrontational. Stress his good qualities.

4. Avoid such negative labels as "alcoholic" or "drug addict."

5. Don't dig up painful events from the past. Focus on the effects of the drug on his actions today.

6. Avoid saying, "You're always drunk." Instead, say, "I've noticed..." or "I'm worried..." or "I'm concerned about you..."

7. Be specific. Say, "I've noticed that you drink almost a full

bottle of wine over the course of an evening."

8. Be direct; treat the elder as an adult. But bear in mind his age and ability to understand.

9. Talk about the effect the drug has on whatever the elder most cares about: his health, his memory, his grandchildren, his religion, his independence.

10. Reduce social isolation. Encourage him to participate in programs that increase mobility and socialization, and that encourage visitors.

11. Expect resistance on the elder's part. Do not force anything he adamantly opposes.

If you suspect substance abuse is a problem, or if you can't deal with the problems effectively, talk to the doctor, visiting nurse, social worker, or a community agency dealing with substance abuse or the elderly. Never handle substance abuse without support and guidance.

Cynthia ─────────────────────

". . .Sometimes she gets days and nights mixed up. They call it the Sundown Syndrome; it's very typical of Alzheimer's patients. She gets noisy at night—her mind starts working, I guess, after she's been docile all day. Sometimes something is bothering her: her nightgown is twisted; she's dirtied herself; she needs a drink, or some sugar-free Jello, or some cereal.

"But if I've tried everything and nothing seems to work, I say, 'Mona, Cynthia loves you.' I've been using her first name instead of Mom because she insists I'm not her daughter—she can be very combative. And I use my name because sometimes it helps her to remember what to call me.

"Anyway, if I've tried everything, I kiss her good-night, close her door, and get a few hours of sleep."

EMOTIONAL DISTURBANCES

11

Generations of families have cared for their elders in the home. Increased longevity, however, now contributes to increasingly stressful family structures, and partly accounts for the wide use of nursing homes.

Alzheimer's disease

Dementia in the elderly has recently received considerable public attention, with Alzheimer's disease being the most common cause of dementia. An estimated 1.5 million people in the United States today have severe dementia. They are so incapacitated that others must care for them continually. An additional 1 million to 5 million suffer from mild or moderate dementia.

Some symptoms of dementia include:

1. Inability to learn new information (impairment of short-term memory)

2. Inability to remember known information (impairment of long-term memory)

3. Inability to find similarities and differences between related words

4. Inability to make reasonable plans to deal with problems

5. Personality changes

6. Inability to work or sustain social activities or relationships due to one or more of the above disturbances

Most patients with dementia are at home, and remain at
home for the major part of their illness—a period that is increasing. Their care is usually provided by family and friends rather
than paid providers.

But the management of dementia in the home is difficult,
and caregiver burden is significantly increased. The caregiver
must understand which reactions are due to the dementia and
learn to handle new and sometimes bizarre behaviors. The goal
is to maximize the elder's quality of life and minimize the caregiver's burden.

Common behavioral problems associated with dementia are:

- Memory disturbance

- Restlessness

- Catastrophic reactions (overreactions to situations or
  tasks)

- Nonspecific agitation

- Day/night disturbance

- Delusions

- Wandering or pacing

- Hallucinations

- Suspicion or paranoia

- Physical violence

- Verbal outbursts (threats, cursing, strange noises)

- Repetitive sentences or questions

- Constant requests for attention

- Complaints, negativism, demanding or critical behavior

- Problems with personal hygiene

- Falling

- Incontinence

- Hiding or hoarding items

- Communication difficulties

- Decreased appetite and difficulty at mealtime

- Verbal or physical sexual advances

- Inappropriate robing or disrobing

- Tearful episodes

- Fearfulness

- Compulsive behavior

- Mood fluctuations

- Unsafe activities: cooking, driving, smoking

The most common dementia behaviors are restlessness, agitation, hallucinations, suspiciousness, incontinence, falling, memory disturbance, and catastrophic reactions. The behaviors reported by caregivers as most serious include physical violence, memory disturbance, incontinence, catastrophic reactions, hitting, and suspiciousness.

Memory impairment is disturbing to both the caregiver and the elder. Typically, short-term memory is more impaired than long-term. For the demented person, life can be described as constantly walking in on the middle of a movie, with no idea of what happened previously.

Restlessness and agitation are problems for about half of demented elders. Typically, they pace, fidget, resist care, or show other irritable behavior. Approaching the elder in a relaxed, friendly manner with a congenial expression is often the key to calming him. He may not fully understand what is said to him, but he is likely to be sensitive to the moods of those around him.

It helps to avoid sensory and environmental overload by keeping his life and the demands on him simple. Common stressors include fatigue, change in routine, excessive demands, overwhelming stimuli, illness, and pain.

Catastrophic reactions by the elder to what he considers a difficult or overwhelming task or situation can unsettle the caregiver, who must realize that the elder's reaction is simply a part of the dementia.

Daytime sleepiness and nighttime restlessness are reported in 40 to 70 percent of demented elders. Wandering occurs in about the same percentage of demented patients who are still ambulatory.

This can be distressing and dangerous—particularly if the elder has day/night disturbance and wanders at night. Making the home safe and secure becomes even more important.

Delusions are similarly found in 40 to 70 percent of demented elders, and are believed to be related in some way to memory loss. Delusions commonly include the belief that "people are stealing from me," that the elder is being abandoned, or is no longer in his own home. Management depends on the severity of the delusion and how it disrupts care. Patience and gentle redirection by the caregiver may be all that is required.

Violence or aggression should be counteracted with distraction, not confrontation. Again, the caregiver should never force an elder—especially a potentially violent elder—to do something he clearly does not want to do. When he must do something—bathe or take medication, for example—the best approach is simply to divert his attention while quickly accomplishing the task, much as you would a recalcitrant two-year-old.

Reduce disturbing behaviors by analyzing when and why they happen, their effect on others, and their effect on the elder. Try this six-step approach to managing behavior problems:

Assessment

1. Describe the disturbing behavior: When does it occur? How often and for how long? What factors precede, increase, modify, and stop the behavior?

2. Identify who is disturbed by the behavior. What feelings are evoked? How does that person react toward the elder?

3. Where does the behavior occur? Who is present? In what environments does the behavior occur and not occur?

4. What are the elder's physical ability, social and psychological status, and medical problems?

Analysis

5. Why is the behavior occurring? What can be changed? Who would benefit from a change in behavior?

Intervention

6. Set achievable goals, choose a plan of intervention, and educate everyone involved in the plan, the goals, and the care of the elder. Re-evaluate the plan after a trial period. If the goals are not being met, try another.

Treatment goals in dementia must focus on the well-being of the elder and the caregiver. The plan must maximize the elder's pleasure, participation in life, autonomy, and security. It must promote physical and emotional comfort and provide dignity and human contact. It must satisfy the caregiver, minimize her stress, and facilitate grieving and acceptance of the elder's illness.

Depression

People over 60 are more likely to suffer from depression than any other age group. When the elderly threaten suicide, they usually mean it. When they attempt it, they usually succeed.

Why? Loneliness is often cited because it is so frequently a part of our elders' lives. But old age encompasses a range of emotional changes, such as anger, irrational fears, and depression. And loneliness can be attributed to so many problems, including physical limitations, loss of friends and family, lost opportunities for socialization, and isolation within the home.

Whatever its source, unrelieved loneliness can turn into depression if the elder becomes withdrawn, apathetic, and negative.

Depression is a potentially serious complication of illness and the elder's most common mental health problem. Depression is a disease with biological, psychological, and social aspects.

The biological aspects include sleep disturbance, loss of libido, and appetite disturbance with possible weight loss.

The psychological aspects include inability to experience pleasure (anhedonia) and sadness (dysphoria), along with guilt and remorse.

The social aspects of depression include withdrawal, elimination of contact with subsequent isolation, and a loss of social functioning.

Depression need not be an inevitable and overwhelming part of old age, but neither is it a rarity. According to the National Institute on Mental Health, 3 percent of Americans over 65 are clinically depressed and another 7 to 12 percent suffer from milder depressions that impair their quality of life. Some elders may have had a lifelong propensity toward depression, but not until late in life does the condition worsen, when situations like retirement, the death of a loved one, or illness trigger it.

It is natural to feel depressed under these circumstances, but when depression persists for months or years it usually has a biological cause as well.

Every serious illness is accompanied by loss. At the very least the patient loses his personal image of invulnerability. At worst he becomes aware of his own threatened immortality. Loss is an often-overlooked reaction to illness.

And every loss brings grief, which is also normal. Grief as a natural response to loss progresses through stages: initial shock or numbness, denial, anger, questioning, bargaining, and acceptance. These stages are predictable, but not linear. They vary with each griever.

Finally, nearly all patients react to illness with fear. This too is natural, certainly when the prognosis is serious. Normally elders respond to fear appropriately, and can contain and manage it. Caregivers need simply to enhance the elder's own normal and natural response.

Illness—which *is* an almost inevitable part of aging—can create depression by altering the brain chemicals that control mood. And any event or illness that produces fear, chronic pain, disability, dependence, or social isolation can trigger depression.

Medication is another major and often overlooked cause of depression. And alcohol, which contributes to depression in people of any age, can be especially destructive to elders.

The elder's reaction to depression can further confuse his family. Depressed people are ashamed of their depression. They believe it will be interpreted by others as weakness of character. Those who have watched an elder sink into depression remark that they initially interpreted it as mental confusion.

An elder with cognitive disorders should not be presumed senile. Nor should his symptoms be written off as an expected part of aging. The person suffering profound grief experiences many of the feelings and symptoms that characterize depression. And some signs of depression, such as memory lapse and difficulty concentrating, mimic symptoms of Alzheimer's disease.

How can you detect depression? If your elder feels low, empty, or down in the dumps for more than two weeks with four or more of the following symptoms, it's probably depression:

- Lack of appetite and significant weight loss
- Sleep disturbances, including insomnia, early-morning awakening, or oversleeping
- Tiredness, lack of energy
- Expressions of pessimism, feelings of worthlessness, guilt
- Indecisiveness, muddled thoughts, inability to concentrate or remember

- Frequent talk and thoughts of death, references to or attempts at suicide

- Irritability

- Recurring aches and pains that do not respond to treatment

While elders are most likely to suffer depression, they are the least likely to recognize or acknowledge it. And too many doctors fail to look beyond physical complaints or ask the probing questions that would reveal depression as the cause of their patients' symptoms.

The doctor may search for a variety of illnesses, find nothing, and turn the patient away with a disheartening, "Sorry, I don't find anything wrong with you." Or the doctor might find an unrelated physical problem and assume it causes the patient's symptoms. The depression remains unrecognized and untreated.

Depression is a real condition. Denying it makes the depressed person feel worse. In its severest form, depression can be life threatening.

Sufferers see suicide as the only escape from a deepening sinkhole of despair. Breaking the elder's sense of isolation is key. You must find ways for him to see and be involved with others. Fortunately, the vast majority of elders—despite the blows they are dealt as they age—do not get depressed as a matter of course. When they do, their lows are temporary and short-lived.

Erik Erikson, the famous psychologist, had his own theory of why some elders are overcome with despair. He believed that the elders who successfully reach and sail through old age have "ego integrity" rather than despair. That is, they fully realize at the later stages of life just who they are and who they have become. They feel they have successfully grappled with the positives and negatives of life to give their life meaning. The successful elder utilizes the past to give meaning to the present.

A lifetime of loving relationships and a sense of purpose make it easier to understand Erikson's theory of "ego integrity." Every elder needs to believe he has earned a place among the generations, and that his life will have a positive bearing on future generations.

Elder abuse

Unfortunately, not all elders achieve ego integrity.

Acknowledging the existence of elder abuse is painful. Elder abuse can range from self-neglect to physical punishment of the elder—usually by a relative in the home. It is difficult to detect because we lack national legal codes, definitions, and reporting requirements. However, statistics indicate that elder abuse occurs in 2 to 4 percent of the elderly population.

Every state describes elder abuse somewhat differently. The following definition comes from the California penal code: "physical abuse, neglect, intimidation, cruel punishment, fiduciary (financial) abuse, abandonment, isolation, or other treatment with resulting physical harm or pain or mental suffering, or the deprivation by a care custodian of goods or services necessary to avoid physical harm or mental suffering."

Physical abuse

Indications of physical abuse include sprains, bruises, malnutrition, poor hygiene, and hair loss due to mistreatment.

Physical abuse can be divided into three categories:

1. **Medical health mismanagement:** inappropriate medication, lack of medication, irregular administration of medication, inadequate access to health care, or the refusal of health care

2. **Neglect by self or others:** dehydration, abuse of alcohol or drugs, and the failure of the elder to thrive

3. **Bodily assault:** sexual assaults, physical restraints, suicidal behavior, battery, and neglect

Neglect is often described as the failure to provide the goods or services necessary to avoid or prevent physical harm, mental anguish, or mental illness. Neglect can be self-inflicted or inflicted by others.

Self-neglect makes up the highest percentage of cases reported to state agencies filing elder abuse reports. Self-inflicted neglect can stem from an elder's decision not to accept services, funds, or medical care. Bear in mind that the patient's right to self-determination is relinquished only if he is declared legally incapable or incompetent. Self-neglect will probably continue to be the abuse most often detected, and the most challenging type for in-home care providers to treat.

Psychological abuse

Psychological abuse is intricately related to other types of elder abuse, as well as to the mental and emotional status of both the elder and the caregiver. It is generally defined as mental suffering deliberately inflicted on an older adult. Humiliation, harassment, and manipulation are examples.

Psychologically abused elders are likely to appear depressed, anxious, and cognitively impaired. They may complain of vague fears, insomnia, helplessness, and hopelessness.

Caregiver stress can lead to elder abuse. The increasing demands for grooming, feeding, bathing, housekeeping, shopping, and money management can overwhelm the caregiver until the stress and resentment are unbearable. Abuse can be the result.

Socially isolated elders are more at risk for abuse than those with good social networks. Isolation makes it more difficult for the elder to reveal mistreatment, and makes it harder for others to notice changes in appearance, behavior, or mental health that may indicate abuse. In general, abused elders tend to have fewer social contacts and are less satisfied with the quality of the contacts they do have than are elders who are not abused.

Misinformation, ageism, and denial on the part of either the caregiver or the elder can relate to elder abuse. A lack of information about the normal physical and cognitive changes of aging, or about medical and nutritional needs, contributes to active or passive elder abuse. Benign neglect, psychological abuse, and financial abuse can stem from limited knowledge or misinformation regarding an elder's needs.

The next chapter provides recommendations for caregivers needing release from the stress of eldercare. If you become concerned about the health or safety of an elder, contact your local authorities.

Regina

There is a determined dignity in Regina Pilhorn's commitment to nurse her mother. She knows no one can do the job she's done, that she alone gives her mother comfort and, occasionally, laughter. And although her children are supportive, Regina doesn't expect them to do for her what she does for her mother. "The modern generation is different," she insists.

But at 58 she feels as housebound as her mother, who is bedridden, blind, diabetic, and has Alzheimer's.

"Just baby-sit for me," she suggests when asked what would make her job easier. "I used to think I needed more skilled help, but not anymore. Now a baby sitter would be just fine. Someone who could warm a meal, do some laundry, even just talk to me. If I had a pleasant person for four hours one day a week, it would help me maintain my sanity. I could take a walk, have a talk, get my mail, start my car—do you know I haven't even started my car in two weeks?"

Caring for both her parents over the past three years, Regina has become the best home care nurse she knows. Twice following hospital discharge she healed bedsores on her parents the doctors thought were nearly impossible. She spends several hours every evening weighing, measuring, cooking, and pureeing her mother's food for the following day. Because she knows just how to turn her mother, she stays home to oversee things whenever a new aide first comes to the house. And she's learned the home care system: how to get information and how to get her mother's needs met.

"You have to listen when the doctor and the social worker come to the house," she advises. "You have to be strong and determined and keep a sense of humor. People give up too fast. I'm not a fighter, but I'm desperate."

Nevertheless, finding and keeping reliable help frustrates her. "I can't afford private care. The county provides 4 hours of health aides three times a week, but the help is unreliable. And Washington has already cut the budget. So someone comes in for two hours to bathe her and give her lunch. Actually, two hours is a nice amount of time. It used to be 45 minutes, and 45 minutes is impossible."

Over the years, Regina has watched her friends drift away. "You know what they say?" she asks incredulously. "They tell me they want to remember my mother the way she was. But what about remembering me?

"People ask, 'What will you do when your caregiving days are over?' They tell me I'm 'overly involved.' But I don't know any other way of life at this point. This is what I have to do now. And I'll tell you, I often think I'd like to volunteer as a caregiver when this is over. People need a lot more education, but I think they would help if they knew about the problems out here. Maybe communities could pay a stipend for volunteer companions, the way we pay Meals on Wheels volunteers.

"There needs to be more public awareness," says Regina Pilhorn. "Think about this: If you volunteer for someone else, maybe someone will be there for you."

CARING FOR THE CAREGIVER

12

Our emphasis up to now has been on the patient. It might seem that he is the only person to be considered, but this is not true. I wrote this book believing that the caregiver, or caregiving family, requires as much care as the patient. In fact, home care does not work unless the entire health care team, including the patient and the caregiver, give the caregiver tender loving care!

No matter how competent, loving, or determined family members may be, the traumatic illness of one member will alter a family's life. The needs of the elder suddenly overshadow all else. The ability of both the elder and the caregiver to cope depends on their respective stages of life and their resultant feelings.

But the key to the success of home care is the caregiver, who often sustains not only the elder but other members of the family, and who mediates between the elder and the outside world.

The primary caregiver must deal with the physical and emotional demands of the elder while helping the rest of the family cope with the stresses that come with change, including a change in everyone's lifestyle, a perceived loss of freedom, and the emotional stress of observing a loved one age and deteriorate physically and/or mentally.

The caregiver family must also bear in mind:

1. The elder may no longer be able to meet earlier expectations.

2. Old conflicts within the family may create new difficulties during crisis situations.

3. Each family member has the right to respect.

A caregiver feels some stress during home care; it is not too much to ask the elder to accept care graciously, avoid excessive demands, and allow the caregiver time to rest.

Intelligent home care planning includes realistic assessment of the energy and availability of the caregiver. For instance, how well can the caregiver adapt to these everyday tasks?

- Administering medications or injections
- Using an oxygen machine
- Tending bedpans and urinals
- Caring for skin, mouth, and throat problems
- Controlling nausea and vomiting
- Seeing to nutritional needs
- Exercising the elder
- Washing and dressing the elder

Caregivers can experience depression while caring for an elder. They may ignore their own needs and become isolated. A regular assessment of the caregiver's coping abilities, by friends or family members as well as by outside professionals, can prevent a crisis situation in which the caregiver needs more care than the elder.

Complex family dynamics can also interfere with efficient, cost-effective home health care delivery. Caregiver burden is well documented, and the burden is not limited to the primary caregiver.

Typically, the caregiver and family accept responsibility for the care of a chronically ill elder for emotional reasons, not because they are proficient at medical treatment. Little information for caregivers is provided by doctors, so the family relies on what they pick up through newspaper and magazine articles, television programs, community agencies, and home health services.

Professional health care services can be a source of conflict as well as help and information. To a health care worker, the patient is the sole focus. The health care worker will not hesitate to suggest that the family spend a disproportionate share of its time, energy, and other resources on the patient.

However, the family sees the elder as but one member of a complex network of people with needs, rights, and responsibilities, all trying to work together for their common good. As time passes and/or the elder's illness progresses, the choice of giving so much of the family's resources to its least productive member is made with decreased enthusiasm. Guilt, resentment, anger, and withholding those fast-depleting resources can be the result. If the burden becomes too great, coping skills break down. Caregiver burn-out may ensue—a disaster for the elder, caregiver, and family alike.

What hardships are most cited by caregivers? And what have they found to be the best solutions?

1. **Night duties**—Try longer-acting drugs, or reduce the mandatory nighttime treatments.

2. **Distressing symptoms**—Educate both the elder and the caregiver, particularly in symptom management. Use preventive therapies.

3. **Fatigue**—Increase the personal time available to the caregiver. Arrange for alternate caregivers. Consider respite care.

4. **Demands on time**—Develop a caregiving network so there is a source of alternative caregivers.

5. **Work disruption**—Communicate with service providers to make appointments prompt and efficient. Make appointments serve multiple functions when possible. Simplify daytime medications and treatments. Use alternative caregivers. Consider a day care center.

6. **Family disruption**—Support the elder's role within the family and urge the elder to support others.

7. **Worries about the future**—Get more information and more education. Hold family meetings at which worries are aired and resolved.

For more information on caregiver support, write:

National Family Caregivers Association
P.O. Box 5871
Capital Heights, MD 20791-5871

Will *home care fit your schedule?*

It's not easy for a busy adult to add eldercare to an already full life. Yet there are ways to revise a schedule to free time for your elder.

Are you employed outside the home? Consider:

1. Temporarily exchanging full-time work for part-time work. Many people are not interested in a full-time job. They gladly share their job with someone with similar abilities and similar interests in part-time employment. Learn how to restructure a full-time job and effectively present the idea to your employer by writing:

   New Ways to Work
   149 Ninth St.
   San Francisco CA 94103

2. Asking your employer if you can use sick days or vacation days to provide care

3. Asking family, friends, or neighbors for help

4. Rearranging work hours

5. Investigating the possibility of working at home

6. Contacting county social services or a social worker for advice about hiring professionals or volunteers

The more stress the caregiver family feels, the poorer the quality of care. While the sheer physical burden can be difficult, the psychological burden can be far worse. The elder's relationship with the rest of the family, the caregiver's health, demands on time schedules, and how chronic illness is perceived by both the elder and the family all have their effects.

Family therapy is often needed to resolve tensions. The goal must be to motivate—or remotivate—the family toward problem-solving rather than emotion-focused strategies, toward seeking information and support from professionals, and toward identifying untapped family strengths and resources.

This is often a good time for home health care workers to intervene, focusing on the entire family. The goal is to identify stress points, poor communication patterns, and lack of information. They can then suggest changes to increase the likelihood of success for the family and the elder. The Watson family is one example.

The Watson family

Arthur Watson was shown deference by his wife and children his entire married life. He was the primary breadwinner, physically the biggest and strongest in the family, with demonstrably superior verbal skills. Clearly, Arthur held the power in the Watson family group.

But following a massive left hemispheric stroke, Arthur lost all the strengths his family had come to expect. During rehabilitation, Arthur was unrelentingly enraged and demanding. Once he threatened his wife, Julia, with a cane when she served him tap water rather than ice water.

Arthur's rage hampered rehabilitation. Home health care professionals could see that although the stroke had destroyed Arthur's capacity to back up his demands for dominance with valuable contributions to the family, he was desperately trying to retain his status. Family therapy helped the Watsons adopt an acceptable redistribution of power. And Arthur's rehabilitation then proceeded more smoothly and successfully.

Problem solving

Different families adopt different problem-solving approaches, which must be considered when home health care is planned.

Is your family an autocracy, in which one authority tells everyone else what to do? Or is yours more of a democracy, with the family making collective decisions? Does your family feel comfortable with professional or outside help? Or are you more likely to withdraw from a problem until a solution is forced by inaction? Do you typically talk about problems as they arise? Do you share feelings?

What about emotional expression? Some families feel no boundaries separating one another, and have little sense of individuality. They don't see one family member as the patient; rather, the entire family is engulfed by the illness. Everyone suffers intense grief, depression, anxiety, and fear. It is hard to find a family member any more functional than the patient.

On the other extreme is the emotionally distanced family. Boundaries are rigid and no one expresses his own feelings, much less feels anyone else's pain. Their problem is loneliness and lack of empathy, with a fear that any attempt to express emotion will distance others even further.

When the family must deal with the emotions and stress of home care, it is futile to believe its problem-solving techniques will differ from what they have always been. There are dozens of family responses to problems, and no intervention can succeed unless the family's unique response is understood and taken into consideration.

Support groups

Sometimes the first step toward relieving the caregiver is a support group, where a caregiver can get new and useful insights into the feelings and needs of her elder and learn options for care. In support groups, caregivers learn coping skills and to make choices based on their needs as well as those of their elder.

Many organizations and hospitals sponsor discussion

groups for family members. These are small sharing groups led by facilitators trained in group or family therapy.

Lay groups—groups without professional guidance—can also be successful. Lay groups choose their own discussion topics, share experiences and techniques, and occasionally schedule experts for new discussions. Such groups exist for mutual encouragement, not as therapy groups. Four to 10 people is a good group size, with a group commitment to a certain number of meetings. If there is no support group in your area, start your own.

1. Make a list of the people you know or know of who are caregivers in circumstances similar to yours.

2. Call each and ask if they would be interested in getting together informally for about two hours. Set a date. Ask each to invite others.

3. Ask a few to bring light refreshments.

4. Start every meeting on time. Begin the first meeting by asking each caregiver to briefly describe his or her caregiving situation. Let each person make this brief introductory statement before beginning the general conversation.

5. Keep the business part of the meeting brief. Allow ample time for members to share and socialize. Focus on caregiving, but otherwise let the conversation take its own course. Each meeting should have one objective, whether it is a special topic or just informal discussion of problems.

6. End meetings on time—after you've established the time and place of second and subsequent meetings.

7. Establish program topics and designate leaders, or hosts, for the next three meetings. If anyone has a contact with a professional or an organization with pertinent information, contact them for future meetings.

8. Keep goals concrete, attainable, and simple. Remember, these people are seeking support because their lives are stressful and full of responsibility—as is yours.

9. Encourage those present to exchange names and numbers, and to invite others if the group is still fewer than nine or ten. New views are the lifeblood of a support group.

Paul

Paul Sylvia was an alcoholic who terrorized his family when he'd been drinking. When, in his mid 50s, the alcoholism finally landed him in a VA hospital, there was nothing left of his family; all but his oldest son had left Paul to his own devices. His liver was so damaged he was not expected to live, but Paul surprised his doctors by pulling through, frail and suffering memory disorders but well enough to be discharged.

But discharged to where? He'd already tried a stint living with his son and his young family, which had been difficult for all.

"He was not ill enough for the VA hospital and not well enough to be out on his own," recalls Paul Jr. So Paul was released to a nursing home, where it soon became apparent that he was well enough to be very angry.

"He acted out," says his son. "He was caught urinating off his balcony. He had a fist fight with his roommate. Finally my wife and I were called in. They told us, 'Maybe this isn't the appropriate setting for your father.'"

When Paul's social worker suggested foster care, an outpatient program of the VA, all agreed. He was placed in a home filled with veterans closer to his age, a definite improvement over the nursing home population for a man in his 50s. But the care seemed callous, the rules were many, and Paul wasn't particularly happy. His son voiced his concerns to the social worker, who agreed to find another foster facility.

The second was in Paul's hometown in Rhode Island, a sprawling old building with an antiques shop in front. The rest of the building was filled with homey furniture, bedrooms and community rooms, a cat and a squawking parrot. There were sheds and additions, a sun porch and a smoking porch, a shady backyard with benches and tables, an institutional-size kitchen, a huge dining table.

The men who ran the home made a point of knowing their roomers' quirks and foibles: One man had a temper, one had to do things in a certain way, another was withdrawn and needed one-on-one attention. In fact, they all got one-on-one attention. The "parents" would cook big meals; they would pile the men into a van for parties or outings.

"It was probably the best of a bad situation," says Paul Jr. "My father liked to go for walks, and could walk into town—the town he'd grown up in. Others were even capable of driving. They definitely weren't under house arrest."

As Paul aged his precarious health deteriorated and he required more and more care. After several hospitalizations, it was determined that he required—and at the age of 65 was more suited for—traditional nursing home care. He died in a nursing home at the age of 75.

"We saw the good and the bad of foster home care," says his son today. "One was crowded and impersonal, and the other was just the opposite. But for my dad, foster care was his chance for independence."

BEYOND THE HOME 13

The two main factors reducing the chance an elder will be admitted to a nursing home are 1) having a spouse or adult child in the caregiving role and 2) having that caregiving relationship in place for a minimum of three years.

Three years is a long time to devote to someone who is probably increasingly dependent and demanding. Who are these selfless people who successfully maintain caregiving over long periods? Do they have more strength, compassion, patience, and time than any of the rest of us?

Hardly. Caregivers able to sustain support for that length of time are not doing so single-handedly. They are simply better at coordinating the multiple services required to meet their elder's needs.

Home health care need not exist solely within the home. Some elders access outside services on a daily basis. Some family caregivers turn to outside services for extra support. Here is a sampling of the services available to caregivers:

Adult day care

According to the National Center for Health Services, day care is a program of services provided under professional leadership in an ambulatory (walking around) care setting. It targets adults who do not need round-the-clock institutional care and yet, because of physical and mental impairments, cannot live independently.

A day care center may be privately or publicly owned, supported by a religious organization, or supported by a private foundation. Elders are referred to the program by their attending physicians, hospital discharge planning program, social service agency, or another source. Day care staff may include nursing assistants, activity personnel, social workers, therapists, registered nurses, and/or physicians.

The goal of adult day care is to maintain and restore health. It offers opportunities to socialize and overcome the isolation often associated with chronic or debilitating illness. Generally, day care offers a wide assortment of services: nursing, nutrition counseling, physical therapy, speech therapy, occupational therapy, physical examinations, social services, personal care, transportation, eye exams, podiatry, patient activities, meals, and more.

In studies comparing the effects of home care combined with day care versus home care alone, elders receiving both improved more than did the home-care-only group.

An 83-year-old man with a fractured left elbow became severely depressed. It appeared likely he would soon require nursing home care. But after being accepted in a day care program that specialized in health care, his improvement was striking. His convalescent time in a skilled nursing facility decreased, he healed well, his spirits soared, and he was able to return to his home care environment and an active life.

The number of day care centers in America has multiplied

tenfold in the past decade, with about 3,000 in existence according to recent estimates. The trend continues to accelerate.

What to look for

Families considering day care for an elder must ask incisive questions, observe carefully, and visit several centers before making a decision. Call the local office on aging, your elder's physician, and/or a social worker and ask for recommendations.

The ideal center offers physical therapy, body movement, music and poetry programs, socialization, and family support. It must offer the elder more interaction and activity than most homes can provide.

Rely on your own observations when you visit a day care center. What is your first impression of the facility? Are there ramps for wheelchairs? Are elders able to relax on the porch or on the grounds? Are programs and materials age-appropriate, including activities that reflect the elder's life experience and interests?

Are medical or therapy services provided? What is the procedure in a medical emergency? Are the premises safe and clean? Is there at least one trained staffer for every six adults? Is the staff trained to recognize medical problems?

Although there is scant data on the effectiveness of day care in serving our aging population, it appears that such programs provide significant relief for caregivers, relieve elder depression, lower medical bills, and delay nursing home placement by an average of 15 to 22 months. In many cases, it eliminates nursing home placement.

Adult day care falls into two broad categories: day hospital programs and multipurpose programs. Day hospital programs are usually affiliated with health care institutions and receive their patients from the institution. They emphasize health care, physical rehabilitation, and treatment, and operate on a fee-for-all-services basis.

Those services can include meals, administration of medication, bathing, transportation, select therapies, socialization, and recreation. They may operate six to eight hours a day and cost the consumer $20 to $50 per day—a fraction of the cost of a nursing home. Medical day care centers may be associated with a church, a nursing home, or a life-care community.

Multipurpose programs do not usually provide rehabilitative care. They focus on patients who are less hampered by illness and more motivated by a need for social interaction and activities. Some social day care programs have a primary medical care and/or preventive medical care program. Social day care is often available at no or low cost, sponsored by government, church, or community agencies.

Day care allows the elder to remain in the family home, avoid institutionalization, and receive the benefits of group activities. A center may be open five days a week from early morning to late afternoon. Fees can be by the day, week, or month. The elder and his family choose the schedule that works for them. The elder gets a change in environment and needed outside stimulus. The family gets a short respite from the burdens of full-time care.

For more information on day care organizations, write

Health Care Financing Administration
Health Standards and Quality Bureau
1849 Gwynn Oak Ave.
Baltimore, MD 21207

Respite care

Respite care (pronounced RES-pit) is a fairly new concept for Americans, but it is popular in Europe as a support service for families of the elderly and disabled. "Respite" means to breathe; it gives family caregivers breathing room in the midst of the taxing job of caregiving. Respite care is the temporary care of an elder for the express purpose of providing relief from the burden of continuous care. Respite care can allow a break of a few hours or even several months.

Respite care can take place in or out of the home. It simply provides a substitute caregiver, affording the primary caregiver some time off. Day care provides respite care, but so can foster homes, board-and-care group homes, and substitute caregivers.

Community services that come into the homes of elders, including chore services, homemaker services, home health services, telephone reassurance programs, volunteer visitors, and home-delivered or nutrition site meals can also provide indirect respite to the caregiver family.

Foster care

The system developed to find homes for abandoned and abused children can also work to keep elders in home settings and in the communities they know.

No statistics indicate how many elders live in foster homes, because no single agency or organization monitors the dozens of programs nationwide. Experts estimate that tens of thousands of elders of varying ages and conditions live in foster homes.

Certainly the numbers are increasing. The government, health policy experts, and families are looking for alternatives that save money and afford the greatest freedom to our elders in choosing a safe and comfortable place to live.

With monthly costs averaging about $1,000—a third of the monthly cost of a nursing home—plus the immeasurable value of living within the embrace of a family, foster care will likely play an increasingly vital role in eldercare.

Foster home candidates are physically able to live with limited supervision but have no family, or their family cannot afford additional help or supervision, or their housing is unsafe or unsanitary. Yet these elders want very much to live in the community, not in an institution. A foster home, while not their own, creates a home where they can be well cared for.

Similar to foster parents for children, foster parents for adults are paid to provide non-related people a home, meals, clean laundry, and a place to sleep. They are also expected to provide a sense of family and watch over the elder. Other services, like skilled nursing, are provided by home health agencies. The elder may pay for his care privately or through a government agency or nonprofit organization.

Often the foster parents own a large house and find they have too much space and too little income. By collecting the monthly fees paid to foster parents, they can hire trained personnel to cook, clean, and help with the personal care of the elders, who must be mentally alert, continent, and ambulatory to qualify for such an arrangement. Well-functioning elders watch television, talk with each other, help with the cooking and housekeeping. They typically leave the home for medical appointments, shopping, entertainment, church, or just a Sunday drive.

Such foster arrangements do not view the elder as a patient. Regulations are kept to a minimum. Meals are family style.

Elders in foster homes, even if they suffer serious medical conditions, focus on wellness, not on their health problems. Foster homes encourage independence. Elders are urged to make the foster home their home and to consider the foster family their family. Quite often, the arrangement provides a family for the foster parent as much as it does for the elder.

There is interest in developing more such mainstream alternatives that permit economies of scale while preserving personal autonomy, control, and privacy. Nursing homes, on the other hand, emphasize illness and the presence of infirmity, which eventually becomes the center of the residents' lives.

There will continue to be a need for nursing homes, but adult foster care is expected to increase to serve a growing population of elders who are not candidates for nursing home care.

Floating bed program

Some day health care programs associated with hospitals offer a bed to an elder for a day or a week if the elder gets sick but does not need to go to a nursing home. The program can also be utilized if the caregiver is sick or hospitalized and can't provide care to the elder for a few days. "Floating beds" may also be available to provide respite for a caregiver.

Mae

Mae Brennan is a psychiatric nurse working for a privately owned home health agency. She's a field supervisor who serves as a liaison between caregivers and the social workers who deal with the elderly.

"The caregivers," she explains, "are busy with the physical aspect of the patient's health, with 'Did you move your bowels?' or 'How is this wound healing?' The social worker talks with the family, organizing community resources, determining what is reimbursable. And we all meet at least once a month to talk about current patients, new patients, and the concerns that arise between meetings. That's often where I pick up leads as to people who need to see me.

"It's probably easier if I just give you an example: A caregiver reported at last month's meeting that the wife of one of her patients had died. Well, a death is a good cue that there needs to be some grief counseling, and that's one of the most important things I do in my job—at least, it's what makes my job worthwhile to me.

"So I made an appointment to see the family. But it didn't turn out to be what I had expected. You see, our patient is a man with Alzheimer's. Although he asked about his wife and was distraught every time he was told she had died, he couldn't remember it. Grief counseling was inappropriate.

"But I noticed that for both appointments I had with him, his daughter made an effort to be there at the same

time. I realized that she was overwhelmed; not only was she grieving for her mother, but for her father as well.

"And it's true: Alzheimer's is harder for the family than for the patient. The patient is really unaware. But this woman was grieving for the father she once knew. It suddenly hit her that both her parents were gone, and it was more than she could handle.

"Now, I talked to her, but technically I can't. I provide reimbursable services to the patient, and I deal with the family only as family issues directly affect the patient. The regulations are very clear, and my employer is very strict about that. My staff knows exactly what constitutes reimbursable services, and the paperwork has to justify everything we do. No nurse likes working that way, but that's the health care industry today, and it gets progressively worse. My bosses fight all the time just to offer the services we do.

"I'll tell you, it makes me think seriously about how well I take care of myself now, while I'm relatively young and healthy, so I won't have to rely on government-paid health care when I'm old. Because I don't think it will be there for us. I see it dwindling every day.

"But as I said, what makes my job worthwhile is the psychiatric nursing, and I do a lot of that. I can't tell you how many people need to hear that it's OK to put their parent in a nursing home. That it's OK to be sad. Or that it's OK to be a caregiver who needs to take time off.

"I've learned so much in this job. I've learned how tough it is to be old and sick, but I've also learned that it's tough to love someone who is old and sick. I meet courageous families every day."

THE FUTURE

We can certainly predict a much greater future demand for eldercare services of a wider scope than have been available in the past. Escalating health costs stimulate that demand, but financial pressure is not the only reason to launch a national commitment to care for elders in their own environments. Home care can no longer be considered merely a segment of the health care system.

It must be viewed as part of a larger social issue. Keeping our elders at home maximizes our sense of human and humane values.

The "graying of America" isn't unique to America. There has been a gradual rise in the median age of most populations. This will continue well into the next century. The population over 60 will grow rapidly after 2010, with the numbers of single elders living alone growing even more dramatically. Those over 70 will increasingly be linked in four-generation families, but they will continue to live separately.

The "future elderly"—those who will be over the age of 60 at the beginning of the 21st century—will have backgrounds and attitudes far different in many respects from their counterparts today, particularly those now over 70. The future elderly are better educated and expect more of themselves and their service providers. They will demand more of the country's social and health systems. In most areas—financial, health, housing, education—the future elderly will be more favorably situated than are the present elderly.

The future elderly have, throughout their lives, demanded and received a higher standard of living, better housing, and an unprecedented barrage of consumer products and options. They have experienced more frequent changes in their family life and had smaller families. The future elderly place more value on housing and will pay higher rents for better accommodations. Most expect to remain in their own homes for as long as possible. They know that, to do this, they will need support from their own social networks.

The rising cost of health care and the fact that the elderly account for over 30 percent of all health care expenditures have widespread implications for the future delivery of health care services in this country. As our society ages and the disability rate escalates, rehabilitation services will become increasingly necessary. The future includes staggering costs—$4 billion to $5 billion a year at today's rates—to treat disabled people in hospitals and other institutions.

My vision for the future of eldercare is fantasy today. But with the unprecedented numbers of Baby Boomers now approaching their 50s, there will soon be the need, the interest, the clout, the finances, and the demand to greatly change the way we perceive and deal with aging. With a firm understanding of the needs of the elderly and a clear vision of what is possible, we will meet—and even exceed—the high expectations of this demanding generation.

Imagine that by the year 2015 there is a successful blending of society, a mixture of old and young, a heterogeneous group of people who live and work together. Imagine that the nursing home concept is gone, replaced by new concepts of self-care.

Perhaps it functions as a campus-style geriatric service center. It acts as a short-term crisis care resource for an elder, who may simultaneously receive long-term support that will allow him to remain in the community. The goal is helping the elder master the prerequisites for daily life in a noninstitutional setting so that he can return to independent community living. It is understood that institutionalization is to no one's advantage.

In this new arrangement, health personnel and each elder decide together what assistance is needed. A new interdisciplinary structure has transformed the outdated nursing home into a health care center with private residential apartments. There is ongoing communication between personnel and the population. The center and its residents are governed by ideas emerging from both groups.

Local centers bring services as close as possible to the elderly population living in the community. These centers handle all social and health issues. All nursing and care benefits are in one facility. There are residents living in the center and visitors who live in their own homes and use the center as needed.

All elders qualify for the same care, whether they live at home or at the center. Staff visit the homes of their outpatients as well, with resources allocated according to need. The old barriers separating institutional and home care services are removed.

The all-important coordination is finally in place, increasing visibility of the center's services. Case managers balance individual client preferences with objective assessment of need.

Each case manager has access to the community's full range of diagnostic specialists and therapies. The homebound and disabled receive increased services, because we have learned that skimping on such services costs society so much in the long run.

Case managers use the center as a centralized intake setting, where varied consulting specialists come to diagnose and provide therapy. The case managers assure continuity of care.

This is a true partnership approach to helping the elderly. It blends the skills of physician; nurse; social worker; technician; pharmacist; nutritionist; home health aide; physical, speech, and occupational therapists; family; friends; and, not least, the elder. Communication within this partnership is the key.

This is a fantasy only if we accept as "good enough" what exists today.

If we accept as good enough elders homebound in fear, depression, and confusion, that's what we'll get.

If we accept as good enough impersonal nursing homes offering undistinguished care, that's what we'll get.

If we accept as good enough long waiting lists for simple geriatric services, that's what we'll get.

If we accept as good enough families at the mercy of unpredictable funding, unreliable services, and an uncompassionate society, that's what we'll get.

What we are getting is not good enough. For the sake of past and future generations, for the sake of our parents, for our own sake, we must recognize that the final stage of life can be—should be—the finest stage of life.

It begins with us.

References

* *A.A.R.P. (1995); Miles Away and Still Caring, Washington, DC.*
* *Amarnick, C. (1995); Healing Chronic Pain, Philadelphia, PA, Aaron Publications, pp 177-181.*
* *Benson, Herbert (1995); The Relaxation Response, New York, NY, William Morrow & Co.*
* *Kauffman, T. (1986); Skeletal Muscle & The Aging Process, Clinical Management in Physical Therapy 6:1, pp 121-123.*
* *Leeson, George (1988); Housing and Services for the Elderly in Denmark—A Private and Public Enterprise, Dane Age Foundation Publications, Copenhagen, Denmark.*
* *Locke S., Colligan D. (1986); The Healer Within, New York, NY, New American Library.*
* *Engel, G.L. (1971); Sudden and Rapid Death During Psychological Stress Ann. Intern. Med. 74: 771-82.*
* *Guzinski, G.M., Murphy, T. (1990); Journal of Clinical Pain Service at The University of Washington Medical Center, Seattle, WA.*
* *Murphy, R. (1982); The Home Hospital, New York, NY: Basic Books.*
* *National Association of Private Geriatric Care, Tucson, AZ.*
* *Peters, A.A. (1994); Leiden University Medical Center, Leiden, The Netherlands.*
* *Platz, M. (1992); Special Dwellings for the Elderly, Danish Medical Bulletin 39 (3) 241-244.*
* *Portnow, J.; Multidisciplinary Home Rehabilitation, A Practical Model, Clinics in Geriatric Medicine, Vol. 7 No. 4, November 1991, pp 695-705.*
* *Seligman, M. (1991); Learning Optimism, New York Alfred Knopf Press.*
* *Tout, Ken (1993); Elderly Care—A World Perspective, London, England: Chapman & Hall Publishers.*
* *Wagner, L. (1992); Non-Institutional Care for the Elderly, Danish Medical Bulletin 39 (3) 236-38.*
* *Weyenborg, Philomeen (1994); Sexual Polyclinic at Leiden University Medical Centre, The Netherlands.*

ABOUT THE AUTHOR

Dr. Claude Amarnick
(1947-1995), doctor
of osteopathy, psychiatry,
and physiatry (physical
medicine and rehabilita-
tion), did extensive
research into the difficulties the elderly face as
their health deteriorates.
His research took him to
Great Britain, Denmark,
and the Netherlands —
countries where govern-
ment, the medical com-
munity, and society as a
whole have taken steps to

ensure that their elderly populations have the best
health care without having to resort to warehousing in
nursing homes and other institutions. On a more personal level, from his home in South Florida Dr. Amarnick
developed a keen sense of the medical and psychological
needs of the elderly population in his own country.

He is the author of **Dr. Amarnick's Mind Over Matter
Pain Relief Program**, a common-sense approach to
managing chronic pain using traditional and holistic

medical techniques. **Dr. Amarnick's Mind Over Matter Pain Relief Program** is also published by Garrett Publishing.

Dr. Amarnick graduated from the University of Pennsylvania, receiving a bachelor's degree in 1969. He graduated from the Philadelphia College of Osteopathic Medicine in 1973. His did his residency in physical medicine and rehabilitation medicine at the University of Pennsylvania, and was board-certified in this specialty. He did his residency in psychiatry at U.C.L.A. Medical Center and at the Beth Israel Medical Center in New York, and was board eligible in this specialty.

Dr. Amarnick served on the medical staff and faculty at the Mount Sinai Medical School in New York, where he taught medical students and house staff about the psychiatric implications of physical disabilities. He developed a reputation among his peers as an expert in chronic pain, and his written protocol for chronic pain management has been utilized in medical facilities throughout the United States. As the director of a much-heralded chronic pain facility in Burbank, California, Dr. Amarnick was interviewed and featured on a week-long NBC series on chronic pain.

Dr. Amarnick was a prolific writer. Along with his own books he contributed a chapter to the medical textbook **Coping With Pediatric Illness: Consultation Liaison Psychiatry**. His professional articles continue to be published posthumously in medical journals worldwide. A partial list follows.

Sexual Abuse & Healing Chronic Pelvic Pain,
Alternative Medical Journal, November/December 1994

Exercise and the Elderly,
The Real Meaning of Relaxation,
Alternative Medical Journal, January/February 1995

"Folk High School,"
Inner Self, April 1995

Spirituality Through Folk High School,
Townsend Letter for Doctors, April 1995

Quest for the Spirit,
Spirituality Through Folk High School,
Alternative Medical Journal, May/June 1995

Sexual Abuse and Pelvic Pain,
Journal of Alternative and Complementary Medicine,
United Kingdom, July 1995

Growing Old is O.K.,
Explore More, August 1995

How You Can Offer a Helping Hand When Signs
of Alcoholism Mirror the Aging Process,
Townsend Letter for Doctors, August/September 1995

Exercise and the Elderly,
Journal of Alternative and Complementary Medicine,
United Kingdom, October 1995

Old Should Not Mean Idle,
**Journal of Alternative and Complementary Medicine,
United Kingdom, October 1995**

Growing Old is O.K.,
Elderly Care,
**Journal of Alternative and Complementary Medicine,
United Kingdom, February 1996**

Range of Feelings,
**Journal of Alternative and Complementary Medicine,
United Kingdom, March 1996**

Alcoholism and the Concerns of the Elderly,
Healing Ministry, June 1996

Index